MW01234808

F.I.G. PUBLISHING

"Write the vision"

All Bible references are taken from the King James Version.
Other references noted and or used are: Gamblers Anonymous
website, *How To Know God* by Deepka Chopra, *Conversations
With God I* by Neale Donald Walsch, and WebMd.com

Published & Distributed by:
F.I.G. Publishing
2760 Cracklerose
Memphis, TN 38127

ISBN 0-9673491-1-7

Library of Congress Control Number: 2004092796

Printed in the United States by:
Morris Publishing • 3212 East Highway 30 • Kearney, NE 68847

Angela Watson

YOU ARE MY SISTER

Words of Wisdom for Conscious Living

Know Thy Self

Anfra

Faith In God Publishing

You Are My Sister

Anfra

To my son

Cameron

A future Meteorologist and Best-selling author

I Love you!

Contents

Contents

Introduction

It is my belief that as human beings, in general, and women, in particular, we have been misinformed, misled, and miseducated in all areas and in all aspects of our lives. And, because of all of this miscommunication, our families, friends, community and we, ourselves, have been mentally pimped and spiritually raped of our God-given rights to live a prosperous and purpose-filled life.

This book and the words within the pages are for opening up a channel of broader vision and deeper thinking. For far too long women have been hurting and have suppressed their pain and discontentment. I believe that if you heal the woman, you can heal the world. Therefore, I hope that as you read this book, the messages are like a medicine or cure for your aching soul. And like any medicine or cure, the only way for it to heal is if you take it and use it wisely.

The objective of the messages within these pages is not to conform you, convict you or convert you to any form of religion or philosophy. The sole purpose of my writing is to make you think. Think about your life and the reason you are here. Therefore, you are free to agree or disagree or even debate what is written. As long as you begin to think, my job as a messenger will be complete. It is my hope that you focus on the messages and *not* the messenger.

Say to wisdom, "You Are My Sister."
Proverbs 7:4

Conscious Living

What is conscious living? We live each day unaware of the rhythm of life. The ebb and flow of life's oxygen is known as love. Conscious living means living in the present while knowingly making constructive choices that determine our future. To live consciously means to be totally aware of every thought, spoken word and action that we take. Conscious means to be alive and aware, therefore responsible and in control of our destiny. However, we are not thinking constantly and therefore make decisions based on reactions rather than thoughts, plans and action.

For instance, with the new technology of cell phones, we are able to communicate anywhere at anytime. Unfortunately, most of us do without thinking about how rude, loud or impolite we are when we're around others. Nor do we "think" about the safety of others or ourselves while we are driving and talking on the cell phone. Why? It is because we are not thinking consciously; we are only reacting to the latest invention.

Moreover, to be conscious means to always think before we react to any circumstance, situation or event in our lives. We should always ask ourselves, "Am I comprising my integrity, dignity and moral decency to do, act, or go a certain place?" More often than not, we compromise all of our moral, social, and personal values everyday in some way.

One of the spiritual principles of conscious living is to always "think before you speak." Most of us never think before we do anything, especially when we speak. We subconsciously live by the motto: "What ever comes up, come out." Some of us are proud of being that way. We don't realize the power of our words and the actions of our body language when we speak.

Most us offend someone everyday with the power of our words and body language. We have to realize that our words have the power to kill someone's spirit, to kill their dreams or to make them commit violent acts upon themselves or someone else.

We've all heard the saying: "The tongue is the most powerful weapon in the world." However, if we consciously think before we speak, our words can also be the most uplifting, encouraging and loving.

The purpose of this book as you read it is to get you to become more conscious in your life. Consciousness is the beginning stage of spiritual awakening. And for far too long, we've been walking around here on earth dead, asleep and unconscious to our own thoughts, words and deeds. After all a conscious woman is a virtuous woman. Are you a conscious woman?

Basic Principles of Conscious Living

- Meditate daily to get in touch with your inner self.
- Always think before you speak.
- Always pray and rely on your intuition and inner voice for guidance.
- Always pay attention to your surroundings and environment.
- Listen and give your undivided attention when engaged in conversations with others.
- Observe how others feel, act and speak.
- Feel the energy of love, understanding and kindness wherever you are and gravitate towards them.
- Take time out to smell the flowers or bask in the sun.
- Always be thankful, polite and kind to others.
- Practice compassion and forgiveness at all times.
- Live in the moment and cherish it.
- Engage only in positive conversations.
- Keep your mind and your body healthy for the body cannot live without the mind.
- Fast or detoxify your body at least once a month.
- Practice non-judgment daily and allow people to live their lives.
- Practice detachment or the art of letting go of expectations and results.
- Don't pollute the earth and the environment around you.
- Start to view life with your spiritual vision.

Divine Discovery

Divine discovery starts with defining first, who you are not and discovering who you are. That self-discovery is the most empowering experience and will change your life forever. It means that no one else has power in your life. Therefore, you can't be promoted, demoted, validated or accepted. Society can't reject you, but will have to respect you for being who you are. Man can't ordain you, contain you, nor restrain you from fulfilling your divine purpose. You won't need approval, nor be denied anything that God has planned for you. You won't need a leader, mediator, or negotiator between you and God. You'll have a daily communion and union with God. Your actions will arrive from listening and communicating with God via solitude, sacrifice and service.

As a result, you'll see clearly with an open mind and heart. You'll turn a deaf ear to society's rules, fashions and trends. You'll give freely and unconditionally. Your highways will become spiritual pathways, and your daily walk of life will be one by faith, not fear. You'll be led by the spirit, give in the spirit, receive in the spirit, and love in the *Spirit of God*.

Now I must warn you. This spiritual awakening will interrupt your present state of living. You'll awaken to a newness of life that you've never experienced before. You'll discover that up to this point, others have controlled your whole life. Things that once seemed so familiar and right will suddenly seem false and unfulfilling. Your spiritual rebirth will cause you to examine all of your beliefs on religion, education, family and career.

Your divine discovery is part of God's divine design and will allow you to live the rest of your life in peace and prosperity. You'll respect God's beautiful universe and be in tune and attuned with the signs of God's divine works. You'll learn to live in synchronicity with God's divine will. Your divine discovery will unite you with other kindred spirits, who are on the same spiritual path of understanding, self-awareness and empowerment. It's time to discover your true-self!

The One

"You are the one that you are looking for."
-    *Audre Lourde-Poet/Author/Activist*

Are you looking for someone to love you? Are you looking for someone to bring you joy and happiness? Maybe you are looking for someone to make your life whole and complete. Well, like the great poetess and social activist Audre Lourde said in many of her speeches and writings, "You are the one that you are looking for."

If you are looking for someone to save you from your troubles, your addictions, and your financial debt – you are the one that you are looking for.

If you are looking for someone to make you happy and to love you unconditionally – you are the one that you are looking for.

If you are looking for someone to send you flowers, to wine and dine you – you are the one that you are looking for.

If you are looking for someone to bring you joy, fun and excitement – you are the one that you are looking for.

You are the one and only one that can love you completely, unconditionally, and unremittingly. All of your life's answers, solutions, and resolutions you have within yourself. YOU ARE THE ONE!

What you look for in others you should see in yourself. What you need from others you should give yourself. What you expect of others you should expect of yourself. What you love about someone else, you should love about yourself. YOU ARE THE ONE!

You are the one with the most power in your life. You have the power to change and control ever aspect of your life. You are your greatest force, source and resource. YOU ARE THE ONE!

Do you want to know why you are the one? It is because you have God's power, the power of unconditional love, supreme health, unlimited wealth and the gift of all knowing. YOU ARE THE ONE!

Therefore, fall in love with yourself. Treat yourself the way you want someone else to treat you. Spend time with yourself and have daily conversations with yourself. Listen to your internal dialogue and follow its divine guidance. Take care of yourself and most of all educate yourself. In other words, get to know yourself. Stand before your spiritual mirror and get butt naked and stripped down to the very core of who you are, and then ask yourself: "Who am I? Why am I here? What is my purpose? What am I doing with my life?"

Do this daily and listen for the answers. In the meantime, educate yourself and become a living, breathing wealth of knowledge. You are going to need it live your purpose and to do your life's work. So get educated, enlightened and empowered because, YOU ARE THE ONE!

Universal Truth

What will the twenty-first century bring to the universe and mankind? First of all, let's look at what the past twenty centuries have brought about — change, knowledge and modernization through technology.

For centuries, man has been seeking the truth about who we are as people, and our relationship to the earth and to the universe. The animals seem to understand it. So do all the elements; that is, earth, wind and fire, as well as all the other planets and stars that make up the universe. But man has yet to understand the complexities of the simple truth. We continuously search for answers to who, what and where God is, when the simple truth is deep inside of us.

The simple truth, no matter what faith or religion we proclaim, is based upon the principles of living, learning and loving. We are living spirits that have taken on the physical body to explore the human experience through learning and loving. All of the trials and errors of this life are to bring us closer to the universal truth of who we are as spiritual beings living in a human body.

Imagine, if you will, God, the all and all, the most powerful Spirit in the universe being like the sun, the largest energy source in the universe. Every particle and ray of sun has the same power as the whole and reaches into every crack and crevice of the universe no matter how small. That's how God is, one powerful Spirit, and we're smaller spirits of the Greater Spirit with the same power of words, hearing, healing, giving and loving on an individual scale.

As we live each day, our ultimate goal should be to discover or learn our universal truth — the truth of who we are spiritually, mentally, and physically, and the assignment or purpose we've been given by God. Neale Donald Walsch, author of the books *Conversations With God*, recorded some of his personal conversations with God. He asked God why do we keep making mistakes? God answered him, "In order to know who you are, you have to experience who you are not. To know what you like, you have to experience what you don't like." It's called living the experience and learning from the mistakes to understand your higher self and greater good.

Upon discovering your truth and living your truth, unconditional love unfolds right before you. You learn to accept people for who they are no matter what rights or wrongs they are experiencing. You will realize that all are one, connected to the same powerful energy source and *all* return to that source after completion of the human experience in this physical plane known as earth.

As you begin to discover your truth, your channel of understanding opens and you make the transition from being a one-dimensional thinker and believer to a multi-dimensional thinker and believer. You are able to accept all faiths and religions as intricate parts of the greater life source and higher power, God. Your judgment of others is removed and replaced with acceptance and love, because you now understand that others are experiencing who they are not on their journey to discovering who they are.

During the next millennium, the world will experience a togetherness and oneness like never before, a coming together of nations, families and cultures via technology and spiritual awakening. This shift of consciousness and unlimited thinking will separate the un-knowledgeable from the knowledgeable. In order to grow and prosper one must know and live their truth. The truth is knowledge and we all know that Knowledge is Power!

What is Your Truth?

What is your truth? Are you living your truth? Can you handle the truth? God's magnificent universe is alive and conscious and honors the truth at all times. Society has abandoned the truth and made it extremely hard for people to live, honor and accept the truth of who we are. We condemn the truth; shame the truth; throw away the truth; hide the truth or simply deny the truth. Peace, happiness, joy, health and wealth are all born of truth. Be true to yourself. Know yourself, honor yourself for this is true love. Know your strengths and acknowledge your weaknesses, for they both represent your truth. Learn to honor your truth by accepting your faults and by continuously striving to perfect and correct them.

Heartache, pain, low self-esteem, anxiety and hopelessness are all offspring of a life not lived in truth. The truth allows pain, wrong doings and bad situations to run their course in time, which brings the truth to the light and rights the wrongs. Healing can only happen once the truth has been revealed. In truth there is freedom, acceptance, empowerment and joy.

We live in a time where it is imperative that we learn to accept the truth of others: our children, our families and people in our communities. For far too long, we have been denied the right to live our truth for fear of being ostracized, ridiculed and discriminated against. Prejudice, hatred and violent crimes are committed because of fear of the truth. What is your truth? What were you born to do or be? How do you find your truth? Only you can only answer these questions. Society judges the truth to be right or wrong, when the truth is simply a fact – *it is what it is.* What is your truth?

To Know God Is To Know Yourself

The world would be a much better place if mankind, choose to know God, not only through religion and conformity, but through freedom, acceptance and unconditional love. To know God is to know the God in you. We are co-creators with God. Most of us know God through our ancestors' and parents' beliefs. We acknowledge God when miracles or disasters happen. We honor God in worship service, praise God in song. We pray to God we we're in need, and thank God when we've been blessed.

We externally know God, yet internally we reject God's holy presence. We want God's spirit to come into our lives as some invisible force, without realizing that God's presence is already within us, waiting to be expressed and revealed. God is not "out there" or in heaven. God is not some thing or some place. God is you. You are God. God is us. God is we. To know God is to create a life for yourself that is based strictly on unconditional love in everything you do, and to know and feel God's presence of love without judgment or organized religion and faith. To understand that everyone and everything needs God's love and you the co-creator can give love without attachment or expectation. When you've reached that realm of understanding and have manifested the love of living, that is when you will know God. It is at this pivotal point in life that you completely know yourself. You know the God in you.

The question is how to know God? The Bible teaches us as much as the people of that era could understand and comprehend about God and the life Jesus. But, as man has evolved, we've learned so much more about the mysteries of God and about the entire universe that God created. It is my opinion and belief that the Bible teaches us to know God externally more than on an internal basis. It teaches about the

God of Moses, the God of Abraham and the Father of Jesus. The Bible also records the life of the children of Israel, and the great prophets David, Paul and John. It is also a rich source of information that teaches about the works of God through an external and one-dimensional point of view. However, we now know and understand that God is so much more that what the great prophets were able to understand, comprehend and write about.

In order to know God we must use the Bible as our first source of reference and layer that knowledge with deep soul-searching, through meditation and surrender. In the book, *How To Know God,* Deepak Chopra, the author, explains the mysteries of God and how to get to know God on a personal level. Deepak explores the mysteries of God and explains how God works within us daily through seven stages and how God reveals himself to us at whatever stage that we are in our lives.

How much about your own life do you know and understand? Do you know why you act and react the way you do about certain things? Do you know what is it that you want out of life? Do you know your reason for being alive? Do you acknowledge your own sense of "all-knowing" or discernment? Have you ever felt that there is more to God and life than what you've been taught by your family, society and religion? Make time in your life to answers these questions and others. Use your power of thought, logic and reasoning in your quest for truth. Learn how to meditate and incorporate your own intuition and prayer into your quest and soon you'll find the God in you.

Obedience Is Better Than Sacrifice

I've been asked time and time again what do I owe my success as a writer and speaker, and what sacrifices did I have make. Like most successful people who pursue their life long dreams and find their purpose in life, I too made a lot of sacrifices. However, it was not the sacrifices, or my walk of faith that changed my life, it was the fact that I decided to obey my higher Spirit and inner voice, which is the voice of God. I quickly learned that obedience is better than sacrifice. It is obedience that warrants success, and honors the Most High. God grants us favors when we listen and obey. For me, being obedient meant writing and speaking out about issues that are seemingly acceptable by our society. Obedience is the highest honor given to God. It is greater than faith, love, trust and sacrifice.

We all make certain sacrifices on a daily basis. We make sacrifices for our children so that they can have more out of life. We sacrifice our health and spiritual well-being to support our families and to help others achieve their dreams. As mothers, we're taught to put ourselves last to keep the family organized and together. As women, in general, we tend to put off our dreams until the children are grown, and the husband has accomplished his dreams. This is accepted as part of our daily sacrifice to support the family.

However, being obedient and listening to God for daily guidance will sometimes run counter to the way women have been trained. More often than not, we have been trained to put everyone else's needs ahead of our own. But in order to be attuned to what God wants us to do, it requires solitude and soul-searching on our parts. This may involve having "time out" for you. Unfortunately, this may be something that your family is not in the habit of seeing. Your spending time alone, nevertheless is a prerequisite to being obedient. For it is when we're still and inactive that God speaks to us and gives us instructions. Those instructions become clear and precise when we're carefully listening. Next, we begin to do God's will. Following God's guidance will change your way of thinking and change directions in your life. Obeying will draw you closer to God and give you strength when family and friends don't understand your change of direction. God gives us inner peace, spiritual fulfillment and assurance that God is with us at all times — that is, when we obey.

❖ Obedience is the safety net that keeps you from falling
❖ Obedience is the stepping stone to success
❖ Obedience is the food on the table when the money is low
❖ Obedience gives you strength when your faith is faltering
❖ Obedience is knowing that God has your back when the bill collectors call
❖ Obedience is the friend that walks with you on your journey alone
❖ Obedience gives you comfort on those cold and lonely nights
❖ Obedience is the preparation for the fruition of your dreams
❖ Obedience lets you smile when troubles occur
❖ Obedience keeps you healthy, happy and in perfect harmony
❖ Obedience is the balance on the scales of life
❖ Obedience keeps you from yielding to temptation and the weakness of the flesh
❖ Obedience protects you from dangers, seen and unseen
❖ Obedience is listening to the voice of God within
❖ Obedience is better than sacrifice.

The Spirit of Giving

An African proverb teaches that the spirit of giving starts with you and touches everyone that is close to you. Once when I was speaking at an engagement in Springfield, Massachusetts, I was taught about an African proverb and the practice of giving. The facilitator asked everyone to form a circle around the room. With your right hand down, and your left hand up, we united hand to hand with the person closest to you. Your right hand that is facing palm down starts the spirit of giving. You should give to the person or people closest to you literally and figuratively. With your right hand, you should give because it's the right thing to do. It is right to give to your love ones first, your family, friends, and neighbors. Next you should give to the people that you come in contact with on a daily basis that need your help. You should give unconditionally and learn to give and to let go, for it is also the right thing to do.

When you reach over the people closest to you to give to other people, places or things, you break the circle of giving. Thus, you break the cycle reciprocity, which means the equal flow or exchange of giving and receiving. Whatever you give or put into the universe with your right hand, give it with love, freedom and without expectations from the person or people that you are giving to. This is called unconditional giving. So often, we give with a grudging heart or with the expectation of receiving something in return from the person that we've given to.

In the Circle, we were asked to give "one dollar," starting with the first person to form the circle. If you give to the person closest to you and let go, the cycle of giving comes back to you from the person standing on your left side with your palm turned up which represents receiving. If you noticed the person that you originally gave to is not the person that gives back to you. The circle of giving is unbroken and complete because you didn't reach over someone close to you and when it was your time to receive you received more than what you originally gave. This is called reciprocity. And reciprocity is one of the spiritual laws of the universe.

While there are religious laws of giving that most of us battle with or have trouble accepting or living by, there are spiritual laws that are universal. These laws and principles are immutable and apply to everyone. No matter what we've been taught, whether it's to tithe or what, the circle of giving works. Make your life a constant practice of giving. Let's stop reaching over our loved ones and people close to us to give to others.

Make a conscious decision to look to your family and loved ones first to see if they need your help. Choose a child or family member that needs help with their children or grandchildren. Make it your life's purpose to start giving. What would the world become if everyone chose to give to their families and loved ones first? I think our families and communities would thrive and prosper because of our unconditional love of giving and helping each other. In turn, the world would become a better place. Despite popular belief, there is not a certain amount, percent or preference when it comes to giving and who better to give to than the people who are closest to you?

One With the Universe

Have you ever paid attention to the splendor of a rising or setting sun? Maybe you've noticed a full moon as it illuminates the night sky. Are you mesmerized at the sight of the stars and how they are shaped to form the big and little dippers? Has a ray of sun ever touched you and made you feel better? Have you ever felt connected to the elements, animals or the moon and stars? Believe it or not, we are all connected and need each other.

Sadly, modern society has become disconnected with the universe where we were created. We've been taught that God made man in his own image. While this is partially true, the image of God is in everyone and everything that God created. Man is not superior or more important than the animals or anything else in creation.

In spite of all of his superiority, man has lost touch with the universe and life's natural energy. Since industrialism and modernization, we no longer rely on the universe to supply our needs. Before this era, our ancestors relied on their intuitive wisdom and used the signs of the moon to plant and harvest the land. However, we no longer cherish the land and pollute the air with toxic chemicals. We kill off the animals and contaminate the soil where the flowers and vegetation grow. The result of our dis-connection has caused our world to become plagued with sickness and disease.

The universe supplies life's natural energy through its natural resources. All of creation is interdependent, which means there is a fair exchange of love, giving, honesty and trust. All of the animals, vegetation, including mankind, need the same natural energy: oxygen to breathe, sun and moonlight to grow and blossom, water and food for nutrition and nourishment. As you grow older and, hopefully, become more spiritual, start to pay attention to the universe. Pay attention to all of the signs it gives you for guidance and conformation. Listen to the birds sing, watch the squirrels as they gather nuts, acknowledge the presence of all of the animals and see them as brethren who cohabit here on earth. Plant some flowers and trees, or grow a garden. Feel the earth between your fingers and learn to appreciate its fertile soil and its richness.

Become one with the universe and rely on its natural energy for good health, sound judgment and moral consciousness. Teach your children to do the same so that they will learn to appreciate the beauty of nature and how to have a reverence for life.

We could save our world if each one of us took the time to reconnect with the universe and it starts by reconnecting to your innate wisdom. Get in touch with your own soul. Filter out the poisons and toxins of mis-education taught by religion, society and family. Start to see God and life from a universal perspective and learn to see the image of God in all things, including yourself. Once you reconnect, you will start to enjoy life and share oneness with the universe. Most of all, you will share a oneness with God.

The Universal Law of Attraction

Have you ever met someone and was immediately attracted to him or her and you didn't know why? Do you ever wonder what draws us to people or why certain people gravitate to us? Have you ever met someone for the first time and felt like you have known him or her your entire life? Do you or someone you know always seem to attract the same type of friends and boyfriends?

Our lives are full of energy and that energy is unique and full of magnetism. Therefore, vibrations we emit into the universe draw other like vibrations. This is called the law of attraction. Innately, we have the power of energy transmission, which means our energy sends out vibrations from our souls and spirits. The energy that transmits comes from our deepest feelings, thoughts and emotions.

For example, do you know someone that no matter where she goes or whom she's with, men always seem to gravitate to her? Why? Most would think it's because of her looks or personality. However, that's not the reason. It's her vibrations that draw men to her.

In relationships, people are able to discern your energy emissions or vibrations. If you are a woman who has to have a man in your life, no matter what, that energy is what you exude and it shows in your actions, body language and conversations. Therefore, you draw unto you men who received your energy vibrations and therefore, you will always have a man in your life. It's not how good you look or any other physical attraction, but simply your vibrations.

Likewise, if you are a woman who does not have to have a man in your life, your energy emissions do not transmit or vibrate that need. Therefore, you don't attract men everywhere you go and it has absolutely nothing to do with how attractive you are.

As spiritual beings we attract the kind of relationships that mirror how we feel about ourselves. If you want to know what kind of person you are, look at the people that you surround yourself with and how they treat you. If you have learned to love yourself, then you won't allow the people in your life to mistreat or to abuse you.

Why? Because your energy vibrations will only attract people into your life that will love you and treat you right. Likeness attracts is the universal law. Those close relationships reflect the kind of person you are. Why? It is because the spiritual law of attraction drew them into your life.

That is why it is so important to understand the law of attraction. Our deepest thoughts, feelings and emotions whether they are positive or negative, attract those feelings, thoughts, and emotions back to us like a boomerang. What you send out is what you receive back.

This universal law of attraction applies to every aspect of our lives. What you think and feel has the power to transform your life. However, we haven't been taught how to use our thoughts, feelings and emotions to become successful in our pursuit of happiness and success. You've heard the saying: "If you think you are sick, you are sick." Moreover, "If you think you are rich, you are rich." Your thoughts and feelings create vibrations that the universe receives and delivers.

So why not start to create a life for yourself that is totally positive, loving and joyous. You have the power and you've already been using it subconsciously. Now is the time to consciously use your thoughts, feelings and emotions to live your best life. If you want to be in love, love yourself first and think positive thoughts about having the love you want in your life. If you want to be wealthy start to think wealthy thoughts and if you want to be healthy think and feel healthy thoughts. Scripture says, "What a man thinks, so is he." What are you thinking?

Sacred Places

Throughout history man has always designated places on earth as sacred and holy. In the Old Testament, Moses walked on Holy Land when he reached the top of Mt. Horeb. There are sacred places that are considered Godly places where the Holy Sprit indwells. Those scared places are kept clean and pure, silent and serene. Scared places in today's civilization since the birth of Christ are sanctuaries, alters, mosques, and temples. These places serve as places of worship and fellowship among believers.

What could be more sacred than the human body? Are these so-called places of worship more sacred than the temple where God's indwelling spirit lives? The body-human was created in the image of God—the creator. An unlike those places that we consider sacred and holy, where we make sure that trash, garbage, or foul language and graffiti doesn't destroy it's integrity and structure—we dehumanize the human body, that very place that embodies the human spirit along with the Holy Spirit.

The most sacred place in the universe is the human body. The human body is the vessel that carries life from the invisible to the visible, from the spiritual to the physical. Its very existence depends upon the invisible element called "breath." It was the breath of God that gave man life and made him a living soul. And it is that same "breath of God" that lives inside of us, yet we destroy and corrupt our temples with foul language, evil thoughts and illicit sex. We dehumanize our bodies with graffiti, tattoos, and body piercing. The temple of God is no longer a sacred placed, but rather a place to make a fashion statement, or a place of evil doings.

Sickness and disease could basically be eliminated if we treat our bodies as sacred places. What you do to your temple, internally and externally determines the existence of the human spirit. Without the Spirit of God, and man, living in harmony within the human body, the physical body starts to deteriorate and decay. A healthy spirit boosts the immune system and rejects infections, diseases and impurities. A healthy spirit also reflects the inner you, therefore it shows physically as well as externally with the things you put on and into your body.

Keeping the human body sacred requires daily nourishment of the mind, body and spirit. Nourishing the mind with positive thoughts, words, and keeping it filled with knowledge allows you to think first before you clothe the physical body. A healthy mind is conscious at all times of the daily functions and activities of the body and careful of what enters into and put on the physical body.

Strengthening the mind opens up channels of understanding and awareness of anything that's a potential danger or threat to the human spirit. The human body serves as a shelter for the spirit and soul. Keeping the body healthy not only keeps the spirit alive, but mirrors the kind of spirit that harbors within. Remember a healthy spirit is a healthy mind and body. Is your mind and body a sacred place?

Think Outside the Box

"It is the world that has been pulled over your eyes
to blind you from the truth."
- The Matrix

We live in a systematic society where people are programmed from the time of birth not to think. Our world has laws, rules, guidelines, borders and boundaries put into place to keep us from using the unlimited possibilities that the universe has to offer. The purpose of this systematic matrix is used to keep us enslaved mentally and spiritually. I guess you can tell I saw the movie, *"The Matrix."* Although this was a fictitious movie with violence and special effects, the philosophical plot was absolutely the truth. The overall meaning of the movie if you didn't get it was to "Free Your Mind," and to "Know Thy Self."

The Matrix that we live in is inside the "box" of thinking—your mind. We've been programmed on how to live by society and through our government that controls our finances, health and wealth. Although slavery was declared unlawful decades ago, and, in theory, we no longer see plantations where slaves worked in the fields from sun up to sun down with little to no pay, there is a new form of slavery still being practiced every day. The new plantation is called Corporate America. The plantation, or "big house," is the corporate office. The fields are the factories, and the slaves are the employees. Employees, black and white and people of all color are the new slaves.

The master-slave mentality still exists and is more profitable than ever before. Why? Because we've haven't been thinking or using our thoughts, logic and reasoning to live our best lives. We live in a reactive mode most of our lives, reacting to what we've been taught and never questioning its teachers. We've been taught to get a good job and work at a company "plantation" until we retire because they offer good benefits. The government "matrix" has set up systems that only allow you to have affordable healthcare and retirement benefits if you work for a corporate plantation.

Another "matrix" that has programmed us to think inside of the box is religion. Most religions teach us to live in fear of God. Why would you fear God is a question I've often asked, but could never get an answer that satisfied my soul. How can you have fear and faith in God and also be taught that fear and faith can't dwell in the same place? But, I digress. We've been taught that God is a vengeful and punishing God that will come back and judge and send us to a fiery hell if we've been living wrong.

Fear is used to keep us oppressed and oppressed people are slaves to their oppressor. We've been mis-educated by religion and, therefore think inside the box "matrix" and never truly experience a loving and autonomous relationship with God.

We've also relied on institutionalized education to provide us with the knowledge that we have on the history of our existence. For example, we truly believe that Columbus discovered America, yet are taught at the same time that the Native Americans were already here when Columbus landed on Plymouth Rock. We never questioned the teachers, the books or people who wrote them. We've just accepted this education, and again, never used our thoughts, logic and reasoning to ask the profound question: How can you discover something or someplace if people were already there when you arrived? Although institutionalized education is good, that doesn't mean that we have to accept or believe everything that we've been taught. We have to learn to question *EVERYTHING!*

Understand that self-knowledge is the most empowering evolution. Learn to study other books, and religions on your own. Incorporate what you read into your own thoughts, logic and reasoning and come up with your own answers, solutions and explanations about life. Learn to agree to disagree with others' opinions and learn from each other's experiences.

When you live and think inside the box "matrix" you live the life of a slave. You are limited in your thinking. Paradoxically, if you decide to think and live differently others judge you. Rather than risk being ostracized, you stay within the boundaries of poverty, unhappiness, religion, tradition, church, and family. And because of this limited way of thinking, your life becomes filled with fear, stress, and depression because you are not mentally and spiritually free. Therefore, you rely on outside sources to fill the empty void in your life. These escapes may include on sex, drugs, alcohol, and gambling, which leads to lust, greed, jealously and envy— all because you are afraid to "free your mind." Your life is inside the box and you need to get out.

Make a conscious decision to think outside the box for happiness and success. Start to think about the strong holds that are keeping you from living your best life, as well as what you need to do to release them. Ask yourself is it your family, religion, job, or relationship that is holding you down. Most of us try to please everyone else and keep our own dreams and ideas to ourselves for fear of rejection. When you start to think outside the box thus begins your journey to happiness, wealth, joy, freedom, peace, prosperity, love and success. It has been said that once your mind conceives a new idea or thought it can never return to its original form. Free Your Mind.

Exercise Your Mind

Do you like to exercise? Most people think of exercise only in the physical sense. While there are various forms of exercise, such as walking, jogging, playing sports, and dancing, exercise is good for the mind as well as the body. Physical exercise helps to relieve stress by allowing oxygen to flow through our vital organs.

Physical exercise requires discipline on a daily basis. When we fail to exercise, the physical body becomes fatigued, overweight and stressed. Slowly, our bodies start to shutdown their vital functions. Without exercise, disease will begin to deteriorate the body. Our lives can become plagued with heart disease, diabetes and other disorders that can eventually destroy our bodies.

No matter how much or how little we physically exercise, most of us very rarely exercise our minds. We fail to stretch beyond the boundaries and limitations of our immediate lifestyles. We don't run with excitement or jog with enthusiasm when we have a new idea or thought. Nor do we race with the opportunity for financial and spiritual freedom.

When we fail to exercise our minds, we stay stagnant, content and even complacent in our lives. The mind is the most powerful tool that we were born with. Nevertheless, we waste it on frivolous things or allow it to become consumed with toxic waste and unhealthy habits. Scientific studies show that most people only use less than one tenth of their brain power during their entire lives. That means that most of us never accomplish anything on our own. We rely on others to think and to make decisions for us.

How often have you had a new idea or thought but failed to "act" or run with it? Then, sooner or later, you see the idea being used by someone else and you think, "That was my idea. I shoulda, woulda, coulda . . ." The opportunity passed you by because you failed to exercise all of the unlimited possibilities needed to bring that idea to fruition.

The fear of success, which is by far greater than the fear of failure, hinders most of us from exercising our minds. Those hideous, "*What ifs*" tend to rob us of potential accomplishments. When you exercise your mind, the first thing you need to do is to learn to let go of fear, self-doubt and disbelief. In essence, you have to believe that you can fly or run the marathon needed to bring your ideas to life. Most ideas or thoughts are divinely inspired. Therefore, the provisions are already made. The only prerequisite that you have to do is exercise your faith and diligently do the work.

Like physical exercise, mental exercise also does the mind and body good. Mental exercise keeps you focused and disciplined. Most of all, it keeps the mind in a positive state. And that positive state is where passion is born, and true passion is true creation. True creation comes only from the true Creator. How often do you exercise your mind?

Daily Mental Exercise

- Stretch beyond your fears, doubts, boundaries and limitations.
- Warm-up with research and exploration on your new idea.
- Walk with the faith that you can accomplish anything you set your mind to.
- Jog with the enthusiasm of giving birth to a new idea.
- Run with the excitement and joy of how the new idea will change your life.
- Remember to breathe as you exercise your mind. Inhale the fresh air of prosperity.
- Pace yourself so that you won't get discouraged and overwhelmed.
- Shake off the "player haters," nay-sayers, and dream killers that surround you.
- Focus only on the positive, keep your head up and always look straight ahead to the future.
- Cross the finish line of success and remember to pass the baton to the people that supported you.

Recommended Books

- *Several Spiritual Laws of Success* – Deepka Chopra – (this book changed my life)
- *Faith in the Valley* – Iylana Vanzant
- *Conversations with God: An Uncommon Dialogue, I, II & III* – Neale Donald Walsch
- *How to Know God* – Deepka Chopra
- *Creating Money: Keys to Abundance* – Sonaya Roman
- *Excuse Me Your Life is Waiting: The Astonishing Power of Feelings* – Lynn Grabhorn

Searching, Running & Hiding

There are three phases of existence that most of us experience during our lifetime. We're searching, running or hiding from God. The majority of our lifetime is spent searching for love, which is searching for God.

From the time we're able to walk and talk, we begin our search for love. We search our parents for acts of kindness, affection and for love. We search our friends and family looking for love. And in relationships, we're constantly searching for love. We search for an Agape love that most of us rarely find in someone else. In our search for love, we want to be accepted and appreciated by our families, friends, boyfriends, husbands or significant others. This search often leads us down the wrong roads because we're following our emotions, and we usually end up on the road of rejection and heartache.

While in the search mode we relentlessly search for external answers to internal problems. We search for religious practices, instead of spiritual resolutions, for what's not working in our homes, families and careers. Our lives continue on a roller coaster of emotional turmoil, mental agony and spiritual emptiness because we're searching in all the wrong places and doing all the wrong things trying to fill a void known as "love – self-love."

Some of us spend an immense amount of our lives running from God. We're no longer searching for love and God, but have found the answer to our life long search. Through many of life's trials and errors, setbacks and comebacks, we eventually stumble upon who we really are. Ultimately, we learn that the greatest love of all is self-love. After years and years of searching once we finally find the real love inside of us, it's more than we want to live up to.

What happens is that God demands more of us when we know who we are, so we start to run from God. We run from love; run from truth; run from our purpose and live in denial as to who we really are. When the search for love is over, the authentic-self cries out to live, to love and to grow. It hungers to experience all that the universe has to offer. While running from God, we run into the evils of the world. Evil is anyone and anything that does not have or know love. We run into the very temptations that bound us to a life of unhappiness.

At some point, as we grow older, we get tired of running. We get tired of searching and tired of running from God, but instead of surrendering to God's will, we try to hide from God's sight. We hide our talents, hide our joys, and hide our true feelings. However, in hiding, we have to be still, be quiet, and slow down our fast pace of life. During this phase, we may stop entertaining the evils, give up the bad relationships and simply stay home in order to hide. Ironically, it is in hiding that God's will overpowers our human spirit. Because we're still and quiet and have closed out the evils, God's omniscient power surrounds and overwhelms the spirit of man. Our inner spirit can no longer hide or deny the presence of God within us. And that Holy Presence is in every one of us, waiting to be liberated.

Whether you're still searching, running or in a hiding state, sooner or later, your life will reach an epiphany, or revelation, which you can't control. That epiphany will change the rest of your life. No matter what age you are when it happens, your entire outlook on life and the world will change. That is when you'll begin to evolve as a higher, more enlightened and spiritual being. You will become more conscious and alive than ever before. Your search will be over. Your marathon completed, and you're no longer hiding in darkness but living in the true and natural realm of spirituality called enlightenment. Are you searching, running or hiding from God?

Make Peace With Yesterday

At the dawn of each glorious day, there is an opportunity for a brighter, better and more bountiful day than the one before. As the radiant sun rises on the horizon of life, it provides a new opportunity to learn from the mistakes we've made or to build on the goals we're trying to accomplish. However, instead of living and enjoying the new beginning, we, more often than not, allow the mistakes, worries and troubles of yesterday to rob us of a wonderful, new and exciting day. We tend to hold on to heartache, betrayal, and abuse. Instead of accepting responsibility for the "victim" role we often played in our own pain, we blame others for our shortcomings.

Until we learn to make peace with the past and allow forgiveness and truth into our present, the past will always steal the joy of today. The past can keep us from planting seeds of success for tomorrow. Make peace with the trials and tribulations of your life and understand that those experiences happened only to make you stronger and to give your life humility, meaning and purpose.

❖ Make peace with your parents. Give them the benefit of doing the best that they knew how, at the time.
❖ Make peace with other family members that you hold a grudge against.
❖ Make peace with the bad choices that you made along your journey of life.
❖ Make peace with the sorrows that destroy your tomorrows.
❖ Make peace with your old boyfriends, who abused you, used you, lied to and cheated on you.

- Make peace with old friends who said something to hurt your feelings or to offend you.
- Make peace with bad habits and throw them into the annals of yesterday.
- Make peace with the blues, depression, and loneliness. Write a new song that's full of life and enthusiasm.
- Make peace with hatred, greed and envy. Get acquainted with love, honor, and respect.
- Make peace with the father that you did not know. Forgive him not being apart of your life.
- Make peace with the mother who put you up for adoption or abandoned you.
- Make peace with those that have betrayed you or done you wrong.
- Make peace with the people you've caused pain and heartache.
- Make peace with your children and spend as much time with them as possible.
- Make peace with your childhood and learn to let it go.
- Make peace with your body and welcome its natural changes. It's part of the progression of life.
- Make peace with old debts and pay them in full.
- Make peace with life and enjoy it to the fullest.
- Make peace with time for it measures your progress.
- Make peace with situations and circumstances that you cannot change.
- Make peace with the elements and learn to appreciate the sun and the rain, for they both have a purpose.
- Make peace with your soul and forgive yourself for all of your mistakes.
- Make peace with death, for it is inevitable.
- Make peace with yesterday!

Misery & Mess

How will you know when your life is finally on purpose? What is your purpose, and how do you know when you're fulfilling it? Well, there's one sure way to know. Have you learned from your past mistakes? If not, then chances are, you're not there yet. How can you tell if your life is a mess? If your bills are still late, your bank account is still in the negative, and you still run from your debtors, then your life has not come full circle. Your purpose is not yet fulfilled.

Are you still hurting from your miseries? Is your heart still broken from past relationships and experiences? Are you still angry with your friends or family members for a wrong that they've done? Are you miserable on your job and still contemplating whether you should quit or work a few more years until you retire? Are you still trying to please people? Is the mess you made out of your life still haunting you and keeping you from being who you are? Do you live day-to-day without a plan? If you answered yes to most of these questions, then you're not on purpose.

God can't use you until you have overcome all of your life's miseries. So, while you're going through your trials of life, your ups and downs and crazy turnarounds, you're being prepared for something greater. All of those disappointments and setbacks are getting you ready for your comeback. All of those tests of faith and courage are getting you ready for your testimony. Those days of heartache and loneliness are getting you ready for love and happiness. Those days of financial debt and poor money management are getting you ready for wealth.

God can't use you until you have cleaned up what you messed up in your life. You have to clean up your relationships with loved ones through forgiveness and learn to move on. You have to clean up your financial debt and clean up your personal life. You have to clean up your temple on the inside and on the outside. God needs to use your whole life—mind, body and spirit. You have to clean up your temple from drugs, alcohol, illicit sex, lies, hatred and envy.

As children, we were taught to clean up our room, clean up the kitchen, and to clean up the house because company is coming. We have to treat our mind, body and spirit the same way, as if company's coming. That company is God.

How will you know when it's time for God to use you?

- When your disadvantages become your advantages
- When your trials become your triumphs
- When your weaknesses become your strengths
- When your downs become your ups
- When your lows become your highs
- When your life goes from powerless to powerful
- When your debt becomes your wealth
- When your battles turn into peace
- When your emptiness becomes fulfillment
- When your hatred turns into love
- When your addictions no longer control you

When your misery becomes your ministry and your mess becomes your message then, and only then, can God use you. That is when you'll live a life with purpose, peace and prosperity.

Out of Order

Is your life out of order? Like a broken-down vending machine or kitchen appliance, does your life need a sign posted on it that reads: *OUT OF ORDER*. Do you ever wonder why bad things keep happening to your life? Or why you haven't acquired wealth or been able to stay in a healthy relationship?

Most of us live our entire lives out of order and don't know it. We need to understand that divine order is what God's universe is governed by. And everything that is in order receives the necessities that are required to survive and to prosper.

What if you were out of order when your blessings came to you? You were some place else and probably doing something that was not right for you. You haven't acquired wealth because you were not in order when it was time to learn the skills needed to save, to invest or to get the right job. You were probably out partying and having fun, instead of studying. Moreover, you haven't met the right man, because when the right man came, you were out with the wrong man.

God has given us everything that we need to live a prosperous, healthy and spiritual life, that is, if only we would get our lives in order. The provisions have already been made for you to accomplish your life's purpose.

When you are out of order, your life is a constant process of bad relationships, financial struggles, emotional despair and spiritual unhappiness. Living out of order is hazardous to your health, family, social and economical happiness because you are relentlessly on a roller coaster of ups and downs. When you are out of order, you usually want to live life "your way."

When your life is in order, it means living your life "God's way." God's way requires you to sit down, slow down, listen, give, love, accept and trust that your life is going to work out fine.

So how do you know if you are out or order? You are out of order if you say you believe in God, but never practice what you say you believe. The way you live your life daily should reflect what you say you believe. You are out of order when you do what feels good, instead of what feels right. There is a big difference between the two. What feels good to you usually is not good for you, and what feels right to you is usually right for you.

When you live life your way, you don't listen to your inner voice, and you're easily persuaded to do things based on emotional needs and instant gratification. Living your way means living spontaneously and making decisions without thinking of the long-term affects that your choices will have on your life. When this happens, your life is out of balance and needs realignment to your spiritual needs.

You are out of order when:
► You live beyond your financial means
► You're in an unhealthy and unequally yoked relationship
► You work at a job that you don't enjoy doing
► You spend money frivolously on things that give you instant gratification
► Your child or children don't respect you
► You use drugs and alcohol to make you feel good
► You don't eat healthy and poison your body with toxins
► You live your life without a plan

As long as your life is out of order, you will continue on the roller coaster ride of extreme highs and profound lows, until something drastic happens to make you wake up. God has a way of getting our attention when we're out of order. And if we start to listen and pay attention, but most of all, start on the path of spiritual enlightenment, soon we'll start to understand. Then, and only then, will we live in perfect harmony and live in perfect peace.

Lucky or Blessed

Are you lucky or blessed? There is a difference. All over the country Casinos and lotteries are a part of our capitalist society. Almost everyone wants to be a millionaire, either by chance, luck or risk. Most people pray to win a Sweepstakes, to hit the jackpot, or to have the winning lottery ticket. Others want to marry a millionaire. There are new game shows, *"Who Wants To Be A Millionaire,"* and *"Greed,"* that have us tuned in each week to see who can win a million dollars. Would winning a million dollars make you happy? Would it give you inner peace and unspeakable joy? How would it change your life? Would you invest it or help your family out? Or would you go out and spend it on trivial things? Moreover, would you gamble with it to try to win more?

Gambling is a growing addiction in our society. It's a hidden problem, and a silent killer that's ruining families everywhere. Why? Unlike drug and alcohol addiction, gambling does not affect your physical condition. It does not impede your corporal productivity, daily activities, nor does it deteriorate your vital organs. However, gambling damages the spirit before it harms the mind and body. It is an addiction that starts out as entertainment, fun and recreation, but before long the human spirit is consumed by greed. The more you win, the more you gamble, and the more you lose the more you gamble to try to win back what you've lost. It's a vicious cycle. That's the hoax that lures you into this silent addiction and just like crack or any other addiction, you can't stop without some form of therapy or rehabilitation.

Casino gambling is a more sophisticated addiction. It attracts a higher "class" of people, mostly people of God. And just like its relatives—drugs, and alcohol—gambling doesn't discriminate and requires a certain belief in luck.

People who believe in luck are willing to take a chance with their earnings and play the high stakes to win. And no matter how much is won, there's so much more lost. Faith in God is lost when one gambles. The faith that God will provide all that's needed and wanted, and the faith to use your earnings to help yourself and others. Most gamblers would rather easily gamble hundreds of dollars and lose, than use their money to strengthen their family, church or community.

Most people who gamble don't see themselves akin to the neighborhood gamblers, who shoot dice on the corner while drinking whiskey and uttering, "C'mon on, seven." Nor do they see themselves being addicted. Drug abusers, alcoholics and gamblers alike live in denial and quickly declare, " I can quit at any time."

Although you may never see gamblers on the street corners begging for their next fix, nor will they rob or kill family members and friends, their addiction is just as serious and affects a larger population of people than crack, alcohol, or heroin. Gamblers are everywhere, in the workplace, church, school and doctor's offices. People are losing their homes and bank accounts to this greed-driven silent addiction.

Being blessed entails a higher sense of responsibility and spiritual awareness. Blessings don't require chance, luck or high risks. Blessings are rewarded when we: trust in God, utilize our talents and give from our hearts. While we continue to labor, we wait patiently to receive them.

God's bank account has millions for everyone. His riches are promised, if only we live by His credit guidelines; the more you give, the more you shall receive. Giving is the principle that blessings are measured. Winning millions of dollars can't buy inner peace, joy, laughter, and happiness. Nor can material riches restore your spirit, and keep you healthy. Having a positive attitude, a giving heart, unconditional love and living by the principles of prosperity enrich the spirit. A rich spirit makes one healthy, wealthy and wise.

People that get-rich-quick have no preparation for the abundance that's thrust upon them. Usually the money is spent, just as fast as it was won. When wealth is acquired through, prayer, planning, knowledge, and sacrifice, there's a sense of appreciation, gratitude and thankfulness that is acknowledged as a blessing, therefore, the wealth is shared and used wisely.

In our society, gambling will always be a deceitful vice— one that leaves us torn between being lucky or blessed, winning or losing, or employment or unemployment. However, the stakes are higher when we chose to take a chance and gamble with our earnings. When someone hits it big and wins a million, someone always loses. If you examine the situation closer, you'll find that even the winner loses something. Are you lucky or blessed?

Gamblers Anonymous offers the following questions to anyone who may have a gambling problem. These questions are provided to help the individual decide if he or she is a compulsive gambler and wants to stop gambling.

www.gamblersanonymous.org/20questions.html

TWENTY QUESTIONS

1. Did you ever lose time from work or school due to gambling?
2. Has gambling ever made your home life unhappy?
3. Did gambling affect your reputation?
4. Have you ever felt remorse after gambling?
5. Did you ever gamble to get money with which to pay debts or other wise solve financial difficulties?
6. Did gambling cause a decrease in your ambition or efficiency?
7. After losing did you feel you must return as soon as possible and win back your loses?
8. After a win did you have a strong urge to return and win more?
9. Did you often gamble until your last dollar was gone?
10. Did you ever borrow to finance your gambling?

11. Have you ever sold anything to finance gambling?
12. Were you reluctant to use "gambling money" for normal expenditures?
13. Did gambling make you careless of the welfare of yourself or your family?
14. Did you ever gamble longer than you had planned?
15. Have you ever gambled to escape worry or trouble?
16. Have you ever committed, or considered committing, an illegal act to finance gambling?
17. Did gambling cause you to have difficulty in sleeping?
18. Do arguments, disappointments or frustrations create within you an urge to gamble?
19. Did you ever have an urge to celebrate any good fortune by a few hours of gambling?
20. Have you ever considered self-destruction or suicide as a result of your gambling?

Most compulsive gamblers will answer yes to at least seven of these questions.

Generational Curses

Now that we've lived through the Y2K scare and have entered a new era that offers unlimited possibilities and opportunities, what did we learn from the 20th century? What emotional baggage and heavy burdens did we bring forth into this new age of spiritual consciousness and cyber technology? As women, we've emerged from being domestic citizens, to being the heads of corporate offices in mainstream America. Many of us have evolved into prominent businesswomen with degrees and positions of power. However, are we utilizing our wealth and economic growth? Are we investing in the future? Or, are we repeating the cycles of poverty, abuse, alcoholism, and the many failed relationships of our ancestors?

In unprecedented numbers, women have climbed the corporate ladder of success and have acquired and accomplished more in our mid-thirties than our ancestors achieved during their entire lives. Yet, unlike the women who came before us, we have more, and love less; we know more and do less; we make more and save less; we spend more and have very little to show for it. And when it comes to relationships, we're repeating the same patterns as our ancestors: our mothers, grandmothers, and great-grandmothers. Like the cycles of abuse and poverty that's passed down generation after generation, so is the cycle of attraction, physical, spiritual or otherwise.

As women, we seem to attract the same kind of relationships that our foremothers attracted. Consequently, we make the same mistakes with men, and usually the same electricity that turned us on in the relationship typically turns us off. This cycle is repeated generation after generation. Sad to say, we're usually unaware of its perilous pattern.

For example: a girl that grows up without her father present and watches her mother date men after men, grows up looking for a father figure in her own relationships. She often repeats the same failed relationships as her mother and those relationships are sometimes abusive. A little girl that sees and knows that her mother dates married men, is usually attracted to married men, and so the cycle continues. Also a young girl that grows up with a loving father in the home often looks for men who will treat her like her father.

The same pattern holds true for men. Boys often repeat the patterns of their fathers (absent or present), or the kind of men their mother's date. These patterns can be broken with the parent's knowledge and awareness of his or her past experiences and behavior, and intercedes with education and a change of dating habits.

Given the fact that people are creatures of habit, these generational curses have held us captive through twenty centuries, and now as we cross the threshold of a new millennium, it's time that we learn to break free of the destructive patterns we've inherited. How? Communication, Self-Evaluation, Determination.

First, we must communicate with our mothers and parents in general to better understand our history and to identify common characteristics, patterns and mistakes in our relationships. Next, evaluate our reasons for dating, by knowing who we are, what we want and more importantly, what we don't want in our mates. Also be determined not to settle for less, no matter what our circumstances are. Most of all, never negotiate self-respect, dignity or intelligence for false intimacy and superficial love.

You Are My Sister

It's time for the sixties and seventies generation of women to break the cycles of poverty, abuse, and failed relationships and pave the way for our young girls who are being led astray. They are following our lead and patterning their lives by our dating ethics. However, our daughters can't afford to pay the price for one wrong choice. With the growing number of HIV & AIDS, our younger generation can't afford to repeat the promiscuous lifestyles that they have inherited. We can't expect them to just know better and do better, unless we set an example for them.

Now is the time for women everywhere to embrace who we are, empower ourselves and set a positive example for the women of tomorrow. Our life changes will not only save, but also set the pace for the next generation.

The twenty-first century holds a promise of prosperity, and peace for anyone who's receptive to change. We all must change from within the destructive traits that rob the future of healthy, responsible and productive human beings. There's a lot to learn from the Twentieth Century; also a lot to be proud of, yet there's so much more we should leave behind.

The Business of Life

Do you own a business? Have you ever thought about owning your own business? Most of us are not business-minded and the thought of being an entrepreneur seems so far-fetched that we usually dismiss the idea as soon and we get it. That profound fear of success and failure usually impedes our dreams and ambitions.

What is an entrepreneur? An entrepreneur is one who organizes, manages, and assumes the risks of a business or enterprise. Also, people that use their talents, gifts and expertise to create a business for themselves are entrepreneurs. While most people think of being an entrepreneur or business owner in the sense of selling a product or service, we all are business owners in the business of life. However, we haven't been taught how to operate or manage the business of our lives.

Let looks at the business of life. Once you become a productive, working adult your life is automatically set up with an account number, which is your Social Security number. That number will be used to track the business of your life until you pass on to the afterlife. Various credit-reporting bureaus will track all of your life's purchases when you purchase homes, cars, or other credit accounts to determine if you are credit worthy and credit reliable. Your life soon becomes a matter of assets and liabilities, debits and credits, savings and investments. And if you are not managing your account to make sure that you are operating in the *black,* your life will soon end up in financial bankruptcy just like any other business that goes under due to lack of poor financial management.

Therefore, life has already been treating you like a business owner. All of your adult life you have been the *Chief Executive Officer* of your own business enterprise. And when you get married your spouse becomes your business partner. And when you have children, buy a house, and a car, those are your assets and liabilities. Your job supplies you with financial stability or income. In turn, the way you manage your finances are your debits, credits, savings and investments. Believe it or not, you have been the CEO of your life and the captain of your ship since you became a decision-making adult.

Like any business, life operates with the same business components. To start a new business the owner must have the following: a business plan, financial plan, marketing plan, business account, insurance, a line of credit, inventory, supplies, and employees or help. In order for the business to succeed the owner has to manage its budget and control spending to make a profit.

Don't we operate our lives in the same manner? If not, we should. First of all, the business of life requires you to have a business plan for your life. That plan is the road map that shows where you are now and where you want to be in future and what it will take to get there. If you live your life without a plan, then how do you know what progress you've made or what it's going to take for you to become successful?

Next, you need a financial plan and marketing plan to track your personal finances. You also need to have a savings, investments and an open line of credit for emergencies or to keep a positive credit rating. And like any business, you need to periodically take inventory of your life and the assets and liabilities that you are managing.

Your marketing plan is the résumé of your life. Your résumé serves as the marketing plan and should include your education, work, experience, training, skills, accomplishments or any other important information that will help you to market yourself for employment with corporations or with other businesses.

Next, you need to take self-inventory to determine if you are truly happy with your life and the progress you have made. You also need to take inventory of the relationships you are involved in to see if they are working for or against your business plan. Those relationships include your spouse if you are married or your significant other if you are not married. You need to determine if your partnership is working and productive. You should also check to see if the two of you are still headed in the same direction. If not, then some re-arranging, consulting and basic communicating needs to happen to make sure that both of you are still interested in being business partners.

Let's face it. Marriage operates entirely like a business. However, most of us go into business with our partners without realizing or knowing if our partner will be a good business partner when it comes to managing the business of life.

Like any business, once you take inventory, you have to determine what you need to keep, what you need to discard or what you need to give away. That inventory adjustment might mean dissolving the partnership or other relationships with friends and family who are not making a positive impact in your life. It might also mean putting out your grown children, or severing ties with people or children who are draining your life financially and emotionally.

Most of us are afraid to take inventory of our lives because we are afraid of what might happen if we do. Taking inventory or stock of our lives can, and will, be a life-changing event and may require a dose of tough love and self-reflection on our parts. However, taking inventory will help to get and to keep our lives on the right track when it comes to our financial, spiritual and emotional well-being.

Finally, in business the sole purpose is to make a profit, which means calculating the net-worth of the business. To do so, a business must add up all of its assets, capital, equity, and investments then subtract its liabilities, expenses and debt. The total sum of this calculation is the net-worth of the business. Hopefully, the total of this calculation is a plus or a profit for the business.

In life, you should do the same. Calculate your net-worth to determine if your life is working for you. You need to determine if you are operating in a plus or minus on your business account of life. Now, I will ask the question again. Do you own a business?

The More Disease

In our western civilization, particularly the United States of American, which is majority Christian by religious principles, is founded in materialism.

The spirit of materialism pervades our society, including the church. We witness this in the way that consumerism and commercialism dominate every aspect of our lives. The constant pursuit of happiness, which is equated to having "more," has spawned a new disease in our society that is spreading faster than any other plague since the beginning of mankind.

The More Disease, as I call it, is being perpetuated by every medium, including religion, politics, education, and health. As consumers, we are enticed to want "more", via the media, which includes television, radio, newspaper and now, the Internet. These are the tools used to spread the "more" virus through advertising.

We've all seen the television shows such as *MTV Cribs*, and BET's *How I'm Living* that showcase entertainer's multi-million dollar homes and expensive cars. Rappers and athletics, who can barely speak Standard English, flaunt their various numbers of expensive cars with designer seats, DVD players and TV's in the headrests and dashboards. The number of expensive cars, homes, and jewelry that they have hanging around their necks defines their happiness and success. Some wear millions of dollars worth of gold teeth, and forget to get braces put on them. This is ignorance at its best. However, we not only love, we worship their lifestyles and try to imitate or duplicate what we see on TV.

The "More" Disease has also contaminated our religious institutions. Our churches and religious organizations now seem to be competing to construct the largest multi-million dollar sanctuaries in our mid-to-low- income communities. Very rarely do you see other religious institutions such as Jewish Synagogues, Muslim Temples or Mosques or any other religious places of worship as large and expensive as our Christian churches.

Sadly, the "More" Disease has taken over most of our churches and their congregations. No matter what service you attend during the week, the main theme of the sermon is to pay your tithes if you want salvation. And let's not forget the importance of the Building Fund. The church seems to always need "more" money it seems to build more buildings, fellowship halls and recreation centers, while the congregation, (its members) owns less than one percent of the businesses in their community. What a tragedy, to spend all of your time, talents and treasure to worship God and never own your own thoughts, let alone your own business.

Yet, we attend faithfully, pay our tithes and have very little happiness and peace in our lives. I've often wondered why can't our churches have Educational Funds, Small Business Funds, Healthcare Funds, Unemployment Funds that are equally as, or more important, than the Building Fund. Unfortunately, the need for more won't allow true happiness and unconditional love into our religious places of worship.

When it is all said and done, does having more make you happy? Let's look at it: The more you consume, the more debt you're in. The more debt you're in, the longer you have to work and the more enslaved you are. After all, debt is bondage and bondage is enslavement. And you thought slavery was over.

As parents we work two and sometimes three jobs to have more and to give our children more. More toys, more designer clothes, more video games and more music so that we can be happy. The more we give our children, the less they appreciate it, and the more they expect from us. The harder we work to have an expensive home the less time we have to enjoy the fruits of our labor. The more money we make, the less money we save and invest for the future. Having more is a continuous and viscous cycle of extreme highs and profound lows.

Why? Because "more" creates a cycle of never being satisfied with what you have. And if you are not satisfied, you are not happy. If you are not happy you constantly want more to make you happy. And the saga continues.

This "More" Disease is the very virus that causes depression, compulsive behaviors and emotional, spiritual and financial bankruptcy. This eventually leads to a life filled with emptiness. Thankfulness, appreciation and gratitude are all consumed and lost to the need to have more.

However, there is a cure for this repulsive disease. If your life has been plagued with the "More" Disease, here are a few simple treatments that will guarantee a complete recovery:

- Be grateful for where you live and take care of what you have.
- Pay your debts in full and don't make any new ones.
- Teach your children how to budget and save money.
- Teach your children to be thankful and how to share.
- Never compete or keep up with your family, friends, neighbors or coworkers.
- Practice giving in all areas of your life.
- Turn off your TV or watch shows that are uplifting and educational.

- Join a church that helps its members to become business owners and critical thinkers.
- Read books about empowerment, spiritual growth and financial management.
- Simplify your life in all areas. This will decrease high blood pressure and eliminate stress.
- Learn to cook and eat healthy.
- Exercise at least three times a week. This will stimulate your creativity and critical thinking.

Don't let the More Disease kill you!

Survive or Succeed

"I shall assure you that distrust is stronger than trust and envy is stronger than adulation, respect or admiration."

- Willie Lynch - West Indies Slave owner

Collectively if you calculate our net worth as families we are multi-millionaires. However, because of the "Willie Lynch" syndrome where our ancestors were taught during slavery to think individually and allow jealously and greed to keep us apart, our families are suffering, even dying, because we fail to support each other.

Who was Willie Lynch? Willie Lynch was a British slave owner in the West Indies who came to the United States in 1712 to teach white slave owners how to keep a slave a slave. He told the slave owners, if you do this, you would keep them enslaved for generations and generations to come. He told the slave owners the way to keep a slave a slave was to shackle their minds, to pitch them one against the another. Teach them fear, distrust and envy which will separate them and one will never have more than the other. He told them to pitch old against the young; the light-skin against the dark-skin one, good hair against the bad hair; house slave against the field slave, female against the male and ultimately, none of them will ever succeed.

Today, over three hundred years later, the slave mentality still exists and Willie Lynch's teachings are still in effect. For instance, if Lil' Johnny is accused of murder, robbery or drug dealing, families will mortgage their homes to get him out on bail, even if chances are he probably did commit the crime. However, if Lil' Johnny wanted to go to college, his family would not come together and mortgage their homes to help him further his education. Why? Because we've been programmed to help each other survive, but we will not help each other to succeed. And there is a big difference between survival and success!

Let's look at other ways the Willie Lynch Syndrome is operative today. Case and point, most of our African American churches operate with the same mentality. If a member gets burned out or experiences some traumatic event the church will raise a special offering or collection to help the member out. However, if the member wanted to start a business there would be little to no financial support from the church. Why? It is because most of our churches will only help you to survive not to succeed.

Take a look at the average African-American community. If you were to do a survey you would find that there is a church on just about every corner or street in the community. Some areas have multi-million dollar sanctuaries sitting adjacent or across the street from each other, while people who don't live in the community own the majority of the surrounding businesses. Those business owners are usually Caucasian, Asian, or Arabs. Yet, our churches are the largest financial institutions in our communities. However, are they using that financial leverage to help its members own the grocery stores, car washes, laundry mats, beauty supply stores and other businesses? That is a question that each and every one of us should ask the religious leaders in our communities.

Our society, family and religious community will only help you to survive not succeed. This is a generational curse that has been handed down since slavery.

You Are My Sister

It is imperative that we, as a race of people, collectively unlearn and stop practicing this Willie Lynch mentality. Most of us never heard of this syndrome. I suggest you do some research on the subject and find out for yourself why we don't support each other.

Take a look around at your family, friends and religious community. Ask yourself a few questions: If you started a business would your family and church help you financially? If your child wanted to go college would they help financially? Also ask yourself would you help support a family or church member start a business or to send their child to college? The answers you get will let you know if you are a victim of the Willie Lynch syndrome. It is time that our families and religious communities break the cycle of poverty and learn not only to help each other to survive, but to help each other to succeed.

Ignorance by Any Other Name ...

Shakespeare was quoted as saying, "A rose by any other name is still a rose." To use the metaphor in a different context, "Ignorance by any other name is still ignorance." What Shakespeare meant was that a rose, with its soft petals and thorns to protect its delicate bulb and sweet smell will always be a rose. No matter what color and name you give it, a rose is still a rose.

Today we call Ignorance by other names to make it acceptable, stylish, mainstream, technical and fashionable. It has been glamorized, glorified, advertised, and personified in every medium possible. It's being sold in every department store and being disguised as designer names and brand names. It is in every industry from telecommunications, books, music, movies and videos.

Whenever ignorance is present, it will always be accounted for, noticed and heard. To be ignorant means to be unaware, uninformed, and uneducated. It also means rude, impolite, inconsiderate or bad mannered.

Ignorance has no dividing line. It crosses all barriers of race, religion and social class. It reins on the rich, as well as the poor. It speaks to and for, the educated and the uneducated. Ignorance travels with the religious and the worldly. Ignorance is not prejudiced or biased. It does not discriminate among its victims. Ignorance speaks every language, yet doesn't know how to properly communicate.

Ignorance has no shame, no humility and no respect or consideration for itself or others. It is boastful, obnoxious and loud. The problem is that ignorance knows no better. Ignorance will wear anything, do anything, say anything. It will take anything yet do nothing about it. This is ignorance at its best!

Ignorance can't be out spoken or defeated. It travels fast and spreads like a virus or disease, and is so easy to please. Ignorance is selfish and self-centered. Ignorance doesn't know when to shut up, get up, or sit down. It always acts like a fool or the class clown. Ignorance will hold center stage in any public place, and if it can't have its way, it'll become violent and throw a rage.

Ignorance is claiming so many lives in our world today. No matter how society dresses it up, promotes, advertises and packages it—Ignorance, by any other name, is still ignorance.

Pro Choice

It is my belief that a woman's body is hers and hers alone to decide what she should do with it, as far as reproduction matters are concerned. For years, I've been a "pro choice" believer when it comes to abortion. I, myself, have had unwanted pregnancies. I have gone through the mental agony and spiritual anxiety of should I keep it or should I terminate the pregnancy. Although I knew one day I would have to face myself, and ultimately God, I made the decision to abort the life growing inside of me.

I had chosen to have unprotected sex and deal with the consequences later. Then, later came, and I regretted the decision. Sad to say, the sexual feeling had long passed, and the sexual partner was long gone. In retrospect, I now know better, and the only regret that I have is that I didn't make the right choice in the first place. The "pro choice" decision to not have unmarried sex, protected or unprotected.

At some point, all women in their lifetime will decide to throw caution to the wind for a few minutes of sexual passion. In that moment of heated spontaneity, we don't want to think about the possibility of disease, let alone the potential concern for life. So often, we make lifelong decisions based upon temporary feelings. It's human nature, an innate trait of our species.

However, as women, we must understand that with every problem, circumstance or obstacle we face each day, we do have a choice—a "pro choice" decision. Bottom line is this: we have an obligation to "think" first in every situation that we find ourselves in, whether it's love, lust, business or otherwise. Every choice we make, consciously or subconsciously, has a consequence that we're responsible for and will have to face the next minute, day, month and year. The choices we make each day affect us for generations and generations to come.

Pro choice simply means the right to choose beforehand; before having unprotected sex; before sleeping with the wrong man; before creating an unwanted pregnancy. Pro choice, or the freedom to choose, will always be a privilege in our world. However, abortions will never go away as long as women continue to use their bodies to fulfill the emptiness and loneliness that plague our lives.

I often wonder what would have happened to my spirit and my gift to the world if my mother had decided to use her "pro choice" right and terminate my life. As my teenage son grows into a beautiful black man, I often wonder what if I had chosen to use my "pro choice" right to abort his life. And what about the beautiful eyes that I will never see because I used my "pro choice" right? For those pregnancies that I chose not to bring into the world, did I terminate the next Michael Jordan, Tiger Woods, Ron Brown, Malcom or Martin? Maybe I terminated the next Oprah, Maya, or Mae Jameison.

Pro choice means to choose. The choice is yours: to choose God over man, responsibility over irresponsibility; patience or spontaneity; respect over disrespect; life over death; love over hate; creation over abortion; spiritual satisfaction over physical satisfaction.

Today, I'm still a Pro-Choice believer, which also means I'm Pro Life.

The Comforter

One night I woke up in the middle of the night extremely lonely and in need of comfort. I wanted to snuggle and cuddle next to a man. It had been a couple of years into my celibacy and I couldn't seem to shake the loneliness. My body ached for the warm embrace and comfort of a man. I wanted to cry, but I couldn't. I began to pray. I prayed that God would take the loneliness away and comfort me. To keep me from making a lonely decision that I would later regret. Before I finished my prayer I fell asleep.

Later that night I felt my ten-year-old son walk into my bedroom and get in the bed with me. I remember feeling his warmth climb into the bed. I never opened my eyes. Instead, I snuggled just close enough to him without touching him. The weight of his body in my bed made me feel good, and I felt comforted and fell into a deeper more sound sleep.

The sound of the alarm clock startled me. It was six-thirty in the morning. It was time for my son to get up and get ready for school. Without opening my eyes, I rolled over and hit the snooze button, then rolled back over to slightly kick him to wake to him, but he wasn't lying next to me. I kicked the covers a little harder because I thought that he might have moved closer to the edge of the bed, but he wasn't there. Finally, I opened my eyes and sat up in the bed to see if maybe he had fallen out of the bed, but he wasn't there. I was sure that he had gotten in bed with me as he sometimes would, except he would never go back to his room. I went to his room to wake him up and he was sound asleep and his bed looked just liked it did the night before. I woke him up and asked him why did he get back in his bed.

With sleep in his eyes, he looked confused and answered the question. "Ma, I didn't get in bed with you."

Hmmm, I thought. "Are you sure?" I questioned.

But it was obvious that he hadn't moved all night in his bed. Puzzled, I walked through the house to check all of the doors and windows to see if anyone came in and got in the bed with me. Everything was in order. However, I felt someone walk into my bedroom, climb into my bed and I snuggled next to their warmth and felt their weight and energy lie next to me. I remembered waking up in the middle of the night feeling lonely and praying for comfort.

Suddenly, God spoke to me and said, "I answered your prayer and sent you a comforter."

I started to cry because I'd never had an experience like that before. The Spirit of God had overwhelmed me and comforted me through the night.

God's Holy Spirit is always present and ready to comfort us, if only we would pray a sincere and unconditional prayer. The Spirit of God can get us through a lonely night. It can comfort us in times of grief, sickness, and loneliness. It can help us through the daily temptations of life.

Close Your Legs and Open Your Mind
"Most requested speech"

A few years ago, I made a conscious choice to stop dating. After years of many failed relationships and maintenance men in my life, I had grown tired of dating, or having sex just to satisfy my physical needs. I wanted and needed something more. I remember clearly the day that I literally threw my hands up in the air and declared, "God, I'm tired. Please keep men away from me. I can't seem to choose the right one. I'll wait on you from now on."

I refused to go to the clubs and parties with my girlfriends. I had long grown tired of going out to the clubs, full of empty people, without a purpose, perpetrating and playing sex games. I was also tired of the "mistress" parties where the married men would come and have fun without anyone knowing. I was also tired of "so called" preachers calling my home, trying to sleep with me.

Every time I turned around, someone I knew was diagnosed with AIDS or was HIV positive. I had no doubt that AIDS was getting closer to my door, and I had to close it before this horrendous disease came in and staked a claim on my life. So, I decided to close my legs, which, ironically, opened my mind.

Years later, I realized that you can't have your legs and your mind open at the same time. When your legs are open, your mind is closed to the truth and peace. It's often been said that love is blind, and that's because your eyes are also closed when your legs are open. When your legs are open to multiple partners and to illicit sex, your life is open and exposed to all forms of illness and disease. It's a scientific and medical fact that most diseases can be detected in a woman's womb with a simple Pap Smear.

Look back in history. Great wars have been fought over a woman having her legs open. Recently, our great nation of America was put to shame, because of a woman having her legs open in the oval office. Kings have been dethroned, and Queens have given up their crown—all because of a woman having her legs open. Women and men are being killed everyday in cases of domestic violence, all because of a woman having her legs open. Some call this obsession "PP" or pussy power.

However, the true "PP" is when a woman refuses to give up her power by keeping her legs closed. When a wife wants or needs her husband to do something, all she has to do is execute her "PP" by closing her legs. Women give up their power each time they open their legs. Men will always conquer our emotions and steal our power as long as we open our legs before we get to really know them and make sure that he is the man God has chosen for us.

What would happen if single or cheating married women decided consciously and collectively to close their legs?

◆ There would be no more babies born out of wedlock.
◆ No more fatherless children
◆ No more AIDS and other STD'S
◆ No more abortions and unwanted pregnancies
◆ No more lying and cheating men
◆ No more White House Scandals
◆ No more cheating in the Pulpit
◆ The divorce rate would drop
◆ No more domestic violence
◆ No more homeless children
◆ No more children on welfare
◆ No more heartache and loneliness

You Are My Sister

When your legs are closed, your mind opens with clarity and understanding. You can see your life clearly as it is at face value. You'll begin to understand why you've been making the wrong choices in all areas of your life. You'll seek the path of personal growth, spiritual transformation, and higher learning. You'll soon learn to love yourself and forgive others who have hurt you.

It is with an open mind that you can hear clearly the voice of God within. With an open mind, God's voice can penetrate your senses, and your life is soon filled with a sense of purpose. And that purpose will bring your life peace and prosperity.

Sisters, close your legs and open your mind. Get those men out of your bed and some knowledge in your head!

Church Ho'
"Second most requested speech"

As Black women, we comprise over eighty percent of our church memberships. We serve on the usher board, sing in the choir, teach Sunday school, and attend Bible study weekly. We are also chairmen of Women's Days, Fashion & Tea Socials, Hat Days, Vacation Bible School and other annual events that the church offers. Most of us attend religious services faithfully and pay our tithes promptly. By all indications, we believe that we are "saved" and have a place waiting for us in heaven because of our attendance, duties and responsibilities to the Church.

I was one of those women who truly believed I was a "saved" woman, based on these righteous duties that I kept to the church. Like most church folk, I also was judgmental of those who I felt were not "saved" because they did not attend or work in the church like I was taught.

However, in the beginning of my spiritual awakening, I started to have many profound conversations with God. These conversations usually were one-on-one during the still of the night. God would wake me up, and we would talk about ways in which God wanted to use my life. I would cry and tell God that I felt unworthy of this calling and that God had made a wrong decision in choosing me. I told God that I was already saved and attended church faithfully. I was doing all that I could do for God. God said to me in my inner spirit, "Let me show you what you've been doing in my name."

God replayed my so-called "saved" life to me in my mind. I went to sleep and God showed me that while I was attending church faithfully, my daily lifestyle was nowhere near the life that I professed. While I attended church and did the duties of the church, I had given the church my time, talent and treasure, but I had failed in giving God my life which included my body. God's exact words to me were, "You've been doing church work, not God's work, and there is a difference."

God's words to me, "You've been a Church whore, because the one thing that honors God the most is your temple."

I cried as God spoke to my life.

God said to me, "How can you give me your life, without giving me your body? I have more respect for a whore in the street because she is being true to herself, than I have for the whores in the church who constantly lie to themselves and do so in my name."

I listened carefully as God spoke to my mind. God's words for my life were these. "Anfra, this is the message that I want you to spread to the women of the church. I want you to tell them that they are not 'saved' until they give their lives to me completely—mind, body and spirit. Tell them that no one can save them, but themselves. They have to make wiser choices and learn to be true to themselves."

I said to God. "God, how can you tell me to say these words to women in the church? They will have me stoned if I get up and tell them about my life and how they too are also whores of the church."

"You go where I send you. Listen to the words that I give you and let me use you. It will be me talking through you. Remember to keep your mind, body and spirit clean. That is the only way that I can use you. Trust me... I know what I am doing."

Sisters, it is time that we stop living the life of a whore, or ho'. We have to stop using our bodies to satisfy our physical needs all while pretending to be saved and sanctified. Our churches are filled with whores and pimps who are preying on others, instead of praying for others. I am confident enough to say and write the words that God has revealed to me to help others who are still lying to themselves.

A saved life is a life where God is first. It has nothing to do with attending church. Church is for fellowship, communion, and learning. Being a faithful servant is how you live your life daily, and, most of all, how you treat your body. If you still smoke, drink, get high, gamble and have illicit sex and still attend church, how are you giving God your life without giving God your body? Are you a Church Ho'?

Bootleg Believers

Have you ever purchased a bootleg CD or movie from someone and you knew it was a bootleg copy? Better yet, maybe you've bought a "hot" dress or suit from a booster, wore it to church, shouted, then became filled with the "Holy Ghost" in your "hot" outfit. I have. ☺ I have to stop and laugh at the silly things I did in the name of the Lord. Whew! Looking back, I was totally ignorant and superficial! I was definitely a bootleg believer.

What is a Bootleg Believer? I'm glad you asked. A bootleg believer is someone who attends church faithfully, pays her tithes faithfully (or occasionally), and who works faithfully in the church. They may even hold various positions in the church. However, the truth of the matter is that they live their daily lives completely contrary to what they profess to believe. A true example of a bootleg believer is a religious believer that bought, sold, downloaded or even watched a bootleg copy of the *Passion of Christ*.

We all know the "Holy Rollers" of the church, the "Thus-said-the-Lord, Bible-toting" saints who will cuss you out, and raise holy hell if things don't go their way. They, too, are bootleg believers. They are bootleg because their actions and lack of self-awareness deem their lives *"bootleg."*

Then you have the regular church-going folks who swear before Jesus and the Father that they love the Lord. Yet, they will buy, sell or trade merchandise on the "Home Boy Hook-up Network." I'm laughing as I write this. I can't help it. These frugal shoppers are always looking for *"something for nothing"* and will go to any lengths to get the best and lowest price. Even, if that means buying or selling hot merchandise, or down right shoplifting to get what they want. And the worst part is that they "Thank God" for the blessing! These faithful shoppers will also argue and fight with other shoppers during the Christmas season just to buy that one special toy or gift on their shopping list.

Now, I must not leave out the faithful and studious believers. You know the ones who attend church faithfully and sleep with every Tom, Dick and Deacon in the church or in the world. You know the church whores that I talked about earlier. I was one of them. Believe it or not, they too are bootleg believers because their promiscuous lifestyles are lived contrary to what they say they believe. I think that covers the majority of the church, except for the children. What do you think?

Oh, I forgot what about those baptized and born-again believers who have illegal cable or satellite TV? They are bootleg too. How about those faithful believers, who smoke more dope than the law allows, but swear up and down that they live a "saved" life? You also have those forty-ounce and half-a-pint believers who get filled with the Holy Ghost on Sundays and filled with the other holy spirits during the week. And don't let me leave out those Sunday go-to-meeting believers who can't wait until church is over to rush to the casino and gamble. Bootleg! Okay! Are you rolling on the floor laughing? I am! ☺

While this message is not meant to judge or hurt anyone's feelings, its only purpose is to bring attention to the discrepancy between how we live our lives and the lies we tell ourselves in the name of the God. It is time that those of us who believe in a Higher Power, Jesus, God or whatever name you want to give the Holy One, to start to live up to our beliefs and religious practices. Or, simply be honest and true to ourselves by admitting that, "I'm not where I need to be in my life." It's time to stop pretending, lying, cheating and doing the "*electric slide*" with our spiritual development. We are only hurting and stunting our own personal, financial and spiritual growth.

Seriously, each time we buy or sell bootleg CD's, movies, or music, we are contributing to theft and copyright infringement. Moreover, we are jeopardizing our own financial freedom. We could also be prosecuted if we're caught buying or selling these items. We have to stop and think, "If I was the artist, would I want people selling my talents and hard work on the down low?"

Remember, what goes around comes back around even harder. If you want to have financial peace and freedom in your life, there are spiritual laws of the universe that you must respect. If you want to one day own your own business, or become an actor or recording artist, then you should respect all art forms. You should also respect and patronize the legal businesses that sell those products. Don't you think the artist should get paid for their hard work and not the bootleggers? Think about it. You would want the same fair treatment if you were an artist or a business owner.

Boosters and shoplifters alike only drive up the cost of the gross domestic product when we buy their "hot" merchandise. Consider this. If you owned a business, would you want shoplifters, boosters, or your employees selling your inventory on the streets? You would not be in business long if they did.

Most of us have been attending church or some religious practice off and on for the majority of our lives, but our spiritual growth hasn't changed from the first day that we claimed we were saved. That means that absolutely nothing about our lives has changed except for our attendance and work inside the church. Why? Because we never take the time to measure or record our strengths and weaknesses, progress or setbacks.

Truthfully speaking, we don't try to grow, and most of have been taught that just attending church and giving our money will save us. This is one pivotal area in our lives where we've been misled and mis-educated by most of our religious leaders. Why do I say this? Because no form of Bible Study, Sunday school or any other Annual Day can teach you the self-awareness and self-control needed to live as an authentic believer. You should have congruency between what you think and say you believe, as well as how you live your life. Unless you incorporate behavioral changes into your regular religious education, you will continue to be a bootleg believer. Being able to quote the Bible and paying your tithes, and shouting every Sunday won't save you, and if it did, what would it save you from?

Remember the spiritual laws of reciprocity. What you give or put into the universe comes back to you good or bad, right or wrong. That is why self-help books, financial workshops, and personal development classes are so important. We all need to learn more about ourselves, and what makes us who we are. That is why I wrote this book, to help you to get to know yourself. So that we can stop living our lives in contradiction to what we truly believe. Once you start to get to know yourself and begin to hold yourself accountable for all areas of your life, then you will start to have the spiritual and financial peace that all of us are searching for. Are you a bootleg believer?

The Sanctity of Marriage

Do you know why most of our marriages end in divorce or why the divorce rate is at an all time high in America? One of the reasons is that people marry for all of the wrong reasons.

Need is usually the driving force that unites most couples in marriage. We marry for the need for love, a need for lust, a need for a helpmate, or a need of comfort. Need is and will always be a temporary lack in our lives. And when that need no longer exists, we no longer need the person or thing that supplies that need. What's left after the need is fulfilled? Discovery. We discover that the person we married no longer fulfills our needs. Therefore, the blinders come off, and we see the person and ourselves for who we really are.

When we're in the first phase of love, most of us might think that we've found the light at the end of the tunnel. Somehow we feel that we were lost until we found the person we've fallen in love with. While this sentiment seems so romantic at first, we soon find out that the light at the end of the tunnel was actually a freight train headed in our direction and will soon run us over. Consider this. If you were lost in your life and someone found and saved you then that person becomes your savior. What does that make you? A victim in need of saving. This sets up the savior/victim dynamic throughout every aspect of the on-going relationship.

That is why it is imperative that when two people take the vows of matrimony, both should be whole and complete. This means the two persons are self-actualized and self-supportive. Therefore, they will be equally yoked mentally, spiritually and financially.

The sole purpose of marriage is for two people who already have a monogamous relationship with God to *share* their love of God together. That is why it is so important for couples to get extensive martial counseling from an unbiased party before they take their vows. Pre-martial counseling will help the couple to evaluate their own lives and the reasons they want to get married. Counseling will also help them to think about the future and to think outside the box on their goals, on their ambitions and, most of all, on their expectations.

In order for marriages to last in our society, we, as friends and family, have to also learn to respect the sanctity of marriage. As women, we have to learn to respect marriage and not allow ourselves under any circumstances to date a married man. We also have to not participate in activities with our friends and family members who are dating married men.

Why? It is because that makes us participants in the adulterous affair. This might seem hard and unfair, but when one of us or one of our friends or family members has chosen to date someone who is married and we participate in their dates, parties, vacations and secret rendezvous, we are cheating too. And marriages will never survive if we don't collectively learn to honor and respect matrimony.

The divorce rate will continue to climb as long as couples who fall in love haven't learned to love themselves above all. Most of us look for someone else to love us and to make us happy. The truth is you have to love yourself and be happy with yourself and your life. You have to already be in love with yourself and happy about where and how you live. You have to already be financially stable and independent.

You Are My Sister

Once of the biggest mistakes that we make when we're in love is that we lose our identity and individualism. We forget who we are and submit to the lifestyle of our partners. We tend to give up our friends, family and other places or things that we once enjoyed before marriage. Over a period of time, we soon lose the most value element we brought to the relationship in the first place — ourselves.

In contrast, a healthy relationship requires two people to have their own thoughts, careers, hobbies, goals and dreams. Although the couple should become one when it comes to the marriage bond, each partner should respect each other's thoughts, careers, hobbies, goals and dreams.

Most couples that get married usually have unrealistic expectations of their relationship. That is because they fail to communicate openly in the beginning, before they get married, what each one wants and expects from the relationship.

Remember the sole purpose is to *share* and not to *need* each other. Sharing is the sole purpose for marriage. We should share the love of God first, and learn to share our joys and happiness, dreams and ambitions and share our trials and tribulations. That is love. Therefore, only the marriages that are equally yoked will survive in our society. Are you equally yoked in your relationship?

Addicted to Drama

Is the relationship you're in full of chaos, fussing, fighting, break-up and make-ups, unfulfilled promises and the "I'm sorry it won't happen again," lies? Is your relationship gauge *"Stuck On Stupid?"* Are you constantly getting signs or messages from God that it's over but you look the other way or simply ignore the signs? You know the signs that God gives when events, people or situations in our lives are wrong. For some of us it's that gut feeling that constantly nags us all of the time. For others, it's those messages on billboards, church marquees, or the sermon on Sunday mornings. You know the messages you read while driving to work or home that read, "Forbidden Fruit Always Creates a Jam," or Practice What You Preach," and Let Go and Let God," and many others.

Our relationships have become so drama-filled and full of confusion that we've become addicted to the daily drama. The sad thing is we don't even know what normal is.

Where there is drama, there are sleepless nights from arguing and sometimes fighting. Drama affects our health, job performance and the lives of our children. However, we tend to confuse the drama with love. "He really loves me and I love him." Let's face it *LOVE DOESN'T HURT*. Nor, does it come with baggage, abuse or drama. We hang on to the drama, hoping and praying that things will change. We hang on to people who are not good for us because of the need to be right, the fear of failure or what others will think. We also do so because of the fear of starting over or the fear of loneliness. Sometimes we hang on for financial reasons or because, "He's my baby daddy."

We also put up with so much drama because we grew up

in dysfunctional, drama-filled families. After all, "Mama didn't leave Daddy and they are still together after years of him drinking, lying and cheating. Daddy changed, why can't my man change?" That's what we try to convince ourselves to stay enmeshed in domestic chaos. Truthfully, we simply lie to ourselves.

In today's world, relationships without drama are a rare find. There's "baby-mama" or "baby-daddy" drama. In some cases, there's more than one "baby-mama" drama to deal with, especially when both parties have different sets of children. There's child support drama, and visitation drama, which creates financial drama to the new household. With stepfamily drama comes the responsibility of who disciplines the children and if the children like the new stepparent.

Lack of trust and jealousy also come with the drama from past relationships where children are involved because the parents should still have constant communication with each other. All of these issues or drama from previous relationships don't give a new relationship a fair chance. However, we try to make it work when, truthfully, it rarely does.

Drama-filled relationships usually happen when two people are not equally yoked. This means they are not on the same level, spiritually and mentally. Usually the only connection they share are physical or sexual. When you are out of balance in a relationship, drama immediately kicks in once the sexual and physical energy starts to dissipate.

Drama, like any other drug, is addictive. We tend to think this roller-coaster existence is normal and expected. Some of us crave and live for this false sense of excitement. Others are blinded by it. In order to live a healthy and productive life, some of us need to be rehabilitated from "drama." Drama in relationships can sometimes become deadly and destructive, if we don't learn to identify its symptoms and learn to get out of it.

You Are My Sister

You know you are in a drama-filled relationship when:

- You argue and fight at least once or more a week.
- You make up with good sex but never talk about or address the real issues that you were arguing about.
- You argue and fight about the same thing over and over.
- You don't trust your partner completely.
- One or both of you deny other addictions, e.g. drug, alcohol, cheating, gambling.
- The only thing good thing between you is the sex.
- You date a married man and accept being second, or third in his life.
- You accept infidelity in any way.
- Emotional and physical abuse seems normal.

If you are in a drama filled relationship, ask yourself the following questions and listen carefully for the answers.

- How can two people, who have no plans for their own individual lives, make plans for a life together?
- How can two people, traveling on different highways, travel through life together?
- How can two people, burdened with truckloads of emotional and financial baggage, carry each other's weight?
- How can two people who don't know how to love themselves love each other?
- How can two people without a purpose find a purpose in life together?
- How can two incomplete people complete each other?
- How can two people, without a dream, dream together?
- How can two people, without God in their lives, see God in each other?

Domestic Violence
"It Could Happen To You"

Never in a million years would I have thought that I would one day become a victim of domestic violence. Like so many young girls who are naive and innocent I thought that if I gave my love to a man, by showing him how much I loved him, he would, in return, treat me right. Boy, was I wrong. I had no idea that a man, for no apparent reason, would cheat on you or physically and mentally abuse you. Although, I must admit, I was being abused and didn't know what abuse was. I didn't know how to tell anyone or how to leave. The psychological affect that men have on women, especially young women, is astonishing.

At the tender young age of twenty, I found myself in love, but in trouble, with the first man that I ever really loved. Over the three years we dated, his abuse slowly progressed until one fateful day in December, just two or three days before Christmas. In a maniacal rage, he beat me beyond recognition. When my parents got to the hospital, they didn't recognize me. They thought the nurses had made a mistake and sent them to the wrong room. When the police officer guarding the door told them that it was me, my mother fell to the floor. Her wailing out loud could be heard all through the halls of the hospital. After they lifted my mother to her feet, the police officer and my father had to escort her back into the hospital room to see me.

I lay there with two extremely swollen black eyes. My lips were swollen and bloody. Blood covered my entire face, which was swollen twice its normal size. My thick long hair had been plucked out in various spots and I could barely hear in one ear. Thankfully, I didn't have any punctures or broken bones, and the hospital released me.

The police officer begged me to press charges, but my abuser had threatened to kill me if I did. He threatened to kill my family or anyone close to me if I pressed charges. He had manipulated my mind for years and I was so afraid of him and what he would do that I didn't press charges. Believe it or not, I was one of those women or young girls at the time that went back to a man who tried to kill me.

At the time of this particular beating, my father stood guard at my bedroom door with a twelve-gage shotgun. In the meantime, all of our neighbors and family conducted a twenty-four-hour vigil on him to keep him from killing my boyfriend. The police officer even told my father, "I understand if anything happens." Surely, to my dad, this event was "A time to kill." It took me years to even talk about my experience. Obviously, I blocked the incident out of my mind.

Anyone at anytime can become a victim of domestic violence. Looking back, my boyfriend had all of the signs of an abuser from the first time that I met him. However, I didn't know the signs. Each year thousands of women die at the hands of their jealous husbands and boyfriends. In retrospect, I could have been one of them.

Here are just a few of the signs. He's probably an abuser if he:

- Always want to know where you've been or even follows you.
- Constantly accuses you of seeing other men.
- Acts jealous when you spend time with your family and friends.
- Threatens you physically if you leave him.
- Always degrades your looks, your weight, and your actions.

- Wants to control what you wear and how you wear your hair or makeup.
- Criticizes your dreams and ambitions.
- Monitors every word you say during conversations with him or with others.
- Accuses you about men in your past, men on your job, or men you see in public places.
- Hits you in places on your body that can't been seen.
- Blames you for making him hit you.
- Cries, begs for forgiveness and promises that it won't happen again, yet it does.
- Threatens to kill you or himself or both if you leave him.
- Threatens to harm your family and friends.
- Forces you to have sex when you don't want to.
- Buys you gifts or treats after he physically hurts you.
- Shows up unannounced at your home, or any other location, to check up on you.
- Destroys your personal property (car, home, clothing, furniture, and jewelry.)
- Have tantrums when he can't get his way with you.
- Abuses drugs and alcohol or other prescription drugs.
- Tries to control your money or secretly reads your bank and credit card statements.

Abusers usually are good lovers sexually, but have an inferiority complex when it comes to intimate relationships. More often than not, abusers witnessed their mothers, grandmothers or other women in their family suffer physical abuse by their husbands or boyfriends. Jealously is usually the driving force behind their abuse. If you, or one of your family members, girlfriends or coworkers, are in an abusive relationship please get out. As concerned sisters we need to know the signs of another sister who is in an abusive relationship. Some of the signs are:

- A sudden change in her personality (quiet, reserved, no longer talkative, etc.)
- She has to rush home or check in with him at all times.
- She has unexplained bruises, scratches, or black eye.
- Absenteeism on her job.
- Talks about him constantly (defends his actions.)
- If you are uncomfortable being around him (this is usually a good sign.)
- Gives up her dreams and ambitions to be with her man.

Are you being abused? Know the signs!

The Change of Life

Turning forty was a milestone in my life. While in my mid-thirties I had set a goal of becoming a best-selling author and motivational speaker. I celebrated my fortieth birthday doing just that. Unfortunately, I didn't plan for the emotional setback known as Perimenopause. Although I knew about menopause, or the "change of life," my only knowledge was that I would someday stop having a menstrual cycle, which I truly looked forward to. However, during my late thirties, I started to have symptoms of what I thought was some sort of emotional distress. I have always been irritable, impatient, and can't stand loud noises or any sort of distractions.

But turning forty, all of those symptoms elevated and I just shut down. I couldn't focus on my writing. I was horny as hell and everything got on my last nerves. My book was selling off the shelves and the requests for the next book were coming from everywhere, yet I couldn't get off the couch and write. I couldn't sleep and I wanted to put my teenage son out and he wasn't giving me any problems.

Finally, I went to the doctor for my yearly exam and explained to my doctor what was going on. When she told me that I was in "Perimenopuase" I wanted to cry.

"I'm only forty dammit!" I protested.

She calmed me down and explained that Perimenopause actually started happening in our mid-thirties and could take years before we loose the dreaded menstrual cycle. I was relieved to know that I wasn't loosing my mind and I started to research Periomenopause to find out why this was happening to me.

You Are My Sister

My doctor wanted to prescribe Zoloft or Prozac but I refused. She also suggested that I take an over the counter estrogen supplement, which I did and gained a tremendous amount of weight afterwards. Needless to say I stopped taking the estrogen.

I found that there are many books, medicines, herbs and holistic practices such as message therapy, yoga, meditation, and other relaxation techniques for those emotional irregularities. I have composed my own list of symptoms that describe what I am going through. As I travel the country I've talked to hundreds of women who are experiencing the same emotional feelings. We laugh and cry together as we gracefully accept our change of life. In the process, we cheer each other up. We know we are not alone.

I want to share with you some of the real symptoms that you might not read about anywhere else. However, don't worry the change of life is normal, but most of us just didn't expect it to happen so early in our lives.

You know you are Perimenopausal if:

Perimenopause – is the transition time between a woman's reproductive years and menopause. Typically, perimenopause occurs between the ages of 40 to 41 (average age is 47,) but hormonal changes may start as early as the late 30's. Emerita®

♦ Suddenly you can't breathe and feel like you want to scream, fight, kick, and die all at the same time. (It's called a panic attack.)

♦ You wake up in the middle of the night dripping wet with sweat. (It's called a Hot Flash)

♦ Your heart palpitates for no apparent reason and you feel extremely anxious.

♦ You're always irritable and can't stand loud noises, people laughing or babies crying.

♦ Your phone rings, you look at the caller ID and don't answer.

♦ Your door bells rings and you look through the peephole at the visitor and don't answer the door.

♦ You want to tell your co-workers, family, and friends to, "Shut the F@!K up!"

♦ You stay in the house all weekend with the blinds closed and don't take a bath.

♦ You wake up in the morning crying and sad, then suddenly, you're laughing out loud.

♦ You call your job and say you're taking the day off and don't lie or give a reason why.

♦ Your whole family gets on your nerves.

You Are My Sister

- ♦ You hate the way you look in the mirror.
- ♦ You have grown a mustache or beard overnight and need to shave.   (It's called hormonal imbalance.)
- ♦ You can't sleep at night and move from the bed to the couch at least ten times during the night.
- ♦ Your bedroom looks like a tornado touched down.
- ♦ Your panties are all in a corner in your bathroom or bedroom and you don't care.
- ♦ Your child or children tell you they are staying out all night and you say "Good, don't come back home at all."
- ♦ You walk into a room and forget what you wanted.
- ♦ You start a sentence and forget what you were about to say.
- ♦ You start several projects and don't finish them.
- ♦ You can't focus on anything productive.
- ♦ You misplace your car keys all the time.
- ♦ You dial a phone number and forget who you are calling.
- ♦ You wear the same outfit twice in one week and don't care.
- ♦ You say what's on your mind and don't care what others think.
- ♦ Your libido or sex drive is so high that you could have sex with the entire U.S. Army or NBA league and not get enough. (Just don't do it!) ☺
- ♦ You look at foreign objects and see them as sex toys.
- ♦ You catch yourself always looking at a man's crotch and wonder how big is his penis.
- ♦ You satisfy your sexual desires and ask God to forgive you and thank Him at the same time! ☺
- ♦ You can't stand being in a crowded room or in a crowd of people.
- ♦ You want to tell your partner/husband/lover/friend that he can't f@!k worth a damn!

- You feel like walking away from everything and everyone in your life and never come back.
- You wear knee high stockings with a dress too short and don't care if anyone sees the band.
- You wish a mugger or robber would attack you because you would f@!k him up!
- You get "road rage" and you're not even driving.
- You go out to eat at a restaurant and ask for the "*no children*" section.
- You comtemplate shooting or posioning your neighbors dog or cat.
- You go off on people for no reason.
- Your family and friends are asking behind your back, "What is wrong with her?"

(I'm feeling real menopausal as I write this. Can't you tell! Woo, it's getting hot in here!! ☺)

Send Me My Flowers

Death is an inevitable event in our lives. It's the one sure thing that will happen to everyone, no matter what race, creed or color. Death doesn't discriminate and is not prejudiced. It is the great equalizer and the ultimate leveler. As people, we view death as the end of human existence. However, to be alive means to be full of energy and energy does not die it simply transforms. Which means only the physical body expires or dies.

It is my opinion that we spend way too much money on funerals and especially on the burial. That is why I want to be cremated. There are so many ways to remember loved ones other than spending thousands and thousands of dollars on a funeral. The average funeral service costs approximately six to ten thousand dollars. Most people never get a chance to spend thousands of dollars on themselves at one time during their entire lives. So why spend that much money when you die? Isn't life more important than death?

The only ones that benefit are the funeral homes and the flower shops. I believe that people should make their funeral arrangements while they are in good health. Think about the money that will be spent and how it could be used to help others instead of spending it all to bury you. Does that make sense? Make your transition into the afterlife uplifting and help to those you will leave behind. You might not want to be cremated like I do. However, the money we spend on funerals could be used to help our children and grandchildren go to college, take music or dance classes. Or, the money could help to set up scholarships, and be donated to organizations that help fight disease, child abuse or any other charitable organization. Why put ten thousand dollars or more into the ground?

Graveyards are already full of people that buried their talents and spiritual gifts that they never used while living. Graveyards are also filled with millions of dollars spent on expensive caskets, plots, and vaults. Why? The human body is biodegradable, which means like the Bible says, "Ashes to ashes... dust to dust," and eventually the body will return to the dust or dirt that we were made from. It's a natural process of the physical body. So why do we preserve it and want to keep if in a grave for eternity?

Also, if you love someone, don't wait until he or she is dead to send him or her flowers. While we are living we should practice the expression of love everyday in some way. If you love someone send him or her flowers while they are living. Make a simple phone call or send an e-card greeting, or post card to show and tell them how much they mean to you. Life is the most beautiful gift, and we should cherish it while we are living. Therefore, send yourself some flowers sometimes. Treat yourself to a nice vacation or dinner with friends every now and then to celebrate your life. Life is for the living, so live your life to the fullest! As the songs says, "Useless the flowers," that you send when someone has already made their transition into the afterlife.

Here's why I want to be cremated:

- I don't want six men to roll me down the isle of the church when I couldn't get one man to walk me down the isle while I was living.

- I don't want those same six men to roll me out of the church, put me in a hole (for eternity) and throw dirt in my face. That's an insult to my beautiful life.

- I don't want people to send flowers of all kinds to my funeral, when no one bothered to send me flowers on my birthday, Christmas, Mother's day or just because while I was living. Besides, when I'm dead I can't see or smell any flowers.

- I don't want ten to fifteen thousand dollars spent on me at one time to bury me when I couldn't go shopping while I was living and spend two or three hundred dollars at one time without putting something in the layaway. (Please don't do that to me.)

- I don't want people getting up for three to five minutes to tell everyone how much they loved me and how much I meant to them and they never bothered to show me how much they loved me while I was living. (I might just get up and slap you if you do that.)

- I don't want to wear the most beautiful dress and corsage to match when I'm definitely not going out on the town dancing with anyone. (I can't even move in a tight casket.)

Anfra Boyd

- After all of my years on earth, the only time that I get to have a make-up artist and hair stylist at my disposal fix me up will be for people to stare at me and say, "She really doesn't look like herself." (Remember me some other way.)

- And please, please... I don't want a preacher delivering my eulogy for thirty to forty-five minutes talking about how good God is or about when Jesus comes back I'm going to meet him in the sky. When I die, my spirit will be set free. So please, please cremate me so that my body will be set free too. I'll see God face to face without all the earthly hoopla and propaganda.

Don't wait until someone you love dies before you send him or her flowers. Tell them how much you love them while they can still hear you. Send them flowers while they're living.

KNOW THYSELF

"Nosce Te Ipsum"

YOU ARE MY SISTER

Know Thyself

Self-help Section

How can you love yourself if you don't know yourself?

How can you be true to yourself if you don't know yourself?

How can you honor yourself if you don't know yourself?

How can you respect yourself if you don't know yourself?

Where are you in your spiritual growth? (check all that apply)

☐   I've outgrown the rituals and traditions of religion and church. I live my life spiritually and have developed my own relationship with God

☐   I still believe that religion and church are the only ways to believe in God and I attend faithfully.

☐   I am tired of religion and church but don't know that else to do at the present time

☐   I believe what I've been taught verbatim by religion, but find it hard to live up to.

☐   I am taking a break from everything and trying to develop my own relationship with God.

☐   I attend church occasionally, more for social purposes, funerals or weddings.

☐   Other: _____

Which one of the following mostly describes you?

☐ Religious – One who believes in God through the rituals and traditions taught by Church

☐ Spiritual – One who believes in a Higher Power or Energy, but is not governed by the rituals and traditions of the church.

☐ Agnostic – One who is not committed to believing in either the existence or nonexistence of God or a god.

☐ Atheist – One who denies the existence of God

☐ Independent Thinker – One who is free to think and believe whatever you want about life as it relates to God or god(s).

☐ Other: _____

If you are a woman who faithfully attends church (1-3 times a month), which one of the following applies to you?

- ☐ I attend faithfully (worship service, Bible study, Sunday School, etc.) and make a conscious effort to live by the scriptures.
- ☐ I attend faithfully (worship service, Bible Study, Sunday School), but I still struggle with sex, smoking weed, gambling, shoplifting, drinking, etc.)
- ☐ I attend faithfully and pay my tithes, but I have yet to give God my body completely.
- ☐ I attend faithfully and I am conscious of my actions everyday. I try to think before I speak.
- ☐ Other: _____

In what ways have you grown since joining church and attending faithfully? (check all that apply)

- ☐ I've stopped dating married men.
- ☐ I've become celibate
- ☐ I've started paying my tithes
- ☐ I've stopped drinking and smoking cigarettes
- ☐ I've stopped smoking weed
- ☐ I've started meditating
- ☐ I am more conscious of my thoughts, words and actions
- ☐ I give more to help my family and friends
- ☐ I've learned my purpose and I am doing it
- ☐ I'm involved more in my community
- ☐ I read more and study God's word
- ☐ I know my strengths and weaknesses

☐   I've learned how to manage my finances
☐   I've stopped gossiping and back biting
☐   I've learned self-control
☐   I no longer steal or shoplift.
☐   I respect myself and others
☐   I've stopping living with men without religious benefit of marriage
☐   I've stopped being homosexual
☐   Other:

_____

What vices do you have?

	Daily	Weekly	Monthly	Occasionally
I smoke cigarettes	☐	☐	☐	☐
I smoke week	☐	☐	☐	☐
I drink beer	☐	☐	☐	☐
I smoke crack	☐	☐	☐	☐
I drink hard liquor	☐	☐	☐	☐
I have illicit sex	☐	☐	☐	☐
I watch pornography	☐	☐	☐	☐
I gamble	☐	☐	☐	☐
I shoplift	☐	☐	☐	☐
Shop (excessively or compulsively)	☐	☐	☐	☐
Other (heroin, prostitute)	☐	☐	☐	☐

Based on the answers above, what areas of your life do you need to make improvements?

1. _____

2. _____

3. _____

4. _____

5. _____

Based on the answers above, what areas of your life that you feel you cannot change or give up doing? Why

1. _____

2. _____

3. _____

4. _____

5. _____

Do you know what your purpose is in life? If so, what is it?

_____

_____

_____

Where do you see yourself in five years?

_____

_____

_____

Where do you see yourself in ten years?

_____

_____

_____

What changes in your life will you need to make to accomplish your goals in the next five to ten years?

_____

_____

_____

Which one of the following best describes you today? (check all that apply)

☐   I have peace in my life and have learned to love myself.
☐   I am still searching for love in all the wrong places.
☐   I am happy with my life, but I still want more.
☐   I feel that I need a man in my life to make me happy.
☐   I am happily married and I still have my own identity
☐   I am married, but my husband and I have outgrown each other.
☐   I am single and celibate.
☐   I am single "save" and still having sex.
☐   I am content without a man.
☐   Other: _____

When it comes to men, which one of the following applies to you most of the time in your life? (Check all that apply)

☐   I have to have a man in my life to feel complete and whole.
☐   I don't have to have a man in life to feel complete and whole.
☐   I have never gone without a man in my life. I am always in a relationship or dating or otherwise.
☐   When I not seeing a man, I am unhappy and don't know what to do with myself.
☐   I lose my identity when I'm in a relationship.
☐   Other: _____

What are some of the lessons that you have learned from intimate relationships? (check all that apply)

☐ I've learned not to have sex right away.
☐ I've learned not to tell a man about past relationships.
☐ I've learned to keep my own identity when dating
☐ I've learned that I can't change a man.
☐ I've learned that we both have to already be whole, complete and happy before we start dating.
☐ I've learned not to date married men.
☐ I've learned that you can't use men for their money or material things.
☐ I've learned not to allow men to use me for money or material things.
☐ Other: _____

How many men have you had sex with in your lifetime? (Be honest)

☐ 1 - 5   ☐ 5-10   ☐ 10-20   ☐ 20-30
☐ 30-40   ☐ 40-50   ☐ 50- 60   ☐ 60- 80
☐ 80-100   ☐ 100-110   ☐ 110-120   ☐ 120- more

Are there any men that you've had sex with that you think might have been bi-sexual?

☐ Yes   ☐ No

Do you know your HIV status?

☐ Yes   ☐ No

You Are My Sister

When a relationship ends which one of the following applies to you?

☐ I take time to heal before I start dating again.
☐ I immediately start back dating.
☐ I quickly have sex with other men.
☐ I wait 3-6 months before I start dating.
☐ I wait 6 months or more before I start dating.
☐ I usually get involved with another man right away.
☐ Other: _____

When involved in a relationship which one mostly describes you?

☐ I allow the man to be the leader and tell me what to do.
☐ I keep up my own identity.
☐ I give up my friends and family once I'm dating.
☐ I keep a balance between my intimate relationship, family and friends.
☐ I change completely to please him.

Which one of the following mistakes have you made most often in relationships?

☐ I seem to keep dating married men.
☐ I seem to always have sex too soon.
☐ I seem to always allow men to live with me
☐ I seem to always get involved with drug abusers
☐ I seem to always get involved with men who are controlling.
☐ I seem to always get involved with men who need my financial help.

☐ I seem to always get involved with men who are violent
☐ I seem to always get involved with men who are alcoholics
☐ Other: _____

When involved in a relationship which of the following applies to you? (check all that apply)

☐ I am usually secure in my relationship
☐ I occasionally feel threatened or insecure by his other female friends.
☐ I am controlling and jealous
☐ I am abusive and violent
☐ I am honest and faithful
☐ I tend to cheat with other men
☐ I am always suspicious of his whereabouts
☐ I occasionally violate his privacy, (check his wallet, pockets, phone calls)

Have you ever had an abortion?

☐ Yes - How many? _____
☐ No

If you had an abortion(s), how do you feel now about having done so?

_____

_____

_____

You Are My Sister

If you knew then what you know now what would you change about your decision to abort your pregnancy?

_____

_____

_____

Have you ever given up a child or children for adoption, if so explain your decision?

_____

_____

_____

When in a relationship which one of the following mostly describes you?

- ☐ Savior complex – I saved my man from his vices—he was lost until he met me—now he's a better man because of me.
- ☐ Victim complex – He saved me from my vices, i.e. debt, unhappiness, and now my life is complete—He is my savior.
- ☐ Father Figure Complex – I like for my man to treat me like a child and I look up to him like a daughter.
- ☐ Mother Figure Complex- I like to treat men like I'm their mother and I date men who are looking for a mother figure to date.

☐ Equal Partnership- I like being treated as an equal partner in my relationship.
☐ Superwoman Complex – I can do it all in a relationship.
☐ Other: _____

What have been some defining moments in your life?

1. _____

2. _____

3. _____

4. _____

5. _____

Name one thing in your life that you know for sure.

_____

_____

_____

_____

_____

_____

How you would describe your sex life today?

- ☐ Promiscuous
- ☐ Virgin
- ☐ Celibate
- ☐ Monogamous relationship

How you would describe your sex life during the last ten years?

- ☐ Promiscuous
- ☐ Celibate
- ☐ Monogamous relationship
- ☐ In and out of several monogamous relationships
- ☐ Virgin

Where are in your sexuality?

- ☐ Heterosexual (secure)
- ☐ Bi-Sexual
- ☐ Openly Homosexual
- ☐ Down Low Homosexual
- ☐ Struggling between heterosexual and homosexual
- ☐ Other: _____

Which one of the following describes you the most?

- ☐ Rebel - one who usually opposes conformity, authority, and prejudice in any form.
- ☐ Follower - One who usually follows the latest trend, fashion or fad.

- [ ] Free Spirit - One who lives life by your own beliefs, thoughts and views.
- [ ] Obedient - One who usually obeys what you are told to do by religion, family, friends, etc.

If you could change one thing about you physically, what would it be and why?

I would change _____

_____

_____

Have you ever been in a physically abusive relationship?

[ ]   Yes   [ ]   No

If yes, how long did you stay in the relationship and why?

_____

_____

_____

Have you ever been raped?

[ ]   Yes   [ ]   No

You Are My Sister

Have you ever been date-raped?

☐　　　Yes　　　　☐　　　No

Have you ever been molested?

☐　　　Yes　　　　☐　　　No

If you answered yes to any of the questions above, write down how you feel and how it has affected your life.

_____

_____

_____

_____

_____

_____

_____

_____

**As of today, what is the most important priority in your life?
(list them by priority)**

____ Continue my education
____ Start my own business
____ Start a family
____ Get married
____ Have man in my life
____ Find my purpose in life
____ Take care of my mental, physical and spiritual health
____ Support my family
____ Support my church
____ Buy a home
____ Find a better job
____ Climb the corporate ladder
____ Have peace and tranquillity in my life
____ End a bad relationship
____ Mend broken relationships

Which one of the following words describes you the most?

☐ Driven
☐ Ambitious
☐ Procrastinator
☐ Incomplete – (start a project or goal but never complete it)
☐ Lackadaisical (lazy)
☐ None of the above

You Are My Sister

What are some of your talents?

1. _____

2. _____

3. _____

Which one of the following words describes you most?
☐ Philosophical
☐ Intellectual
☐ Wise
☐ Courageous
☐ Empowered
☐ Spiritual
☐ Uninhibited
☐ Enlightened
☐ None of the above

What levels of consciousness are you involved? (check all that apply)
☐ Political
☐ Social
☐ Religious
☐ Environmental
☐ Family
☐ Educational
☐ Heath
☐ Spiritual
☐ Community
☐ Economical
☐ None of the above

What are most of your conversations about? Listen to yourself when you talk with others before answering.

- ☐ My child or children
- ☐ My husband
- ☐ Men in general (always talk about having, finding or losing a man.
- ☐ Material things (how much something cost, who's the designer, what's on sale)
- ☐ Empowerment conversations
- ☐ Spiritual conversations
- ☐ Negative conversations
- ☐ Gossip (he say, she say)
- ☐ God (every other word, is God this... or the Lord that)
- ☐ Money (how much who's making, who's got what, etc.)
- ☐ Diverse conversations
- ☐ Job
- ☐ Other: _____

When a close friend, relative or someone in general calls you do you:

- ☐ Answer and immediately start talking without giving the person on the other end a chance to say what or why they are calling.
- ☐ Answer and listen to what the caller has to say without interrupting.
- ☐ Talk to other people and try to listen to the caller at the same time.
- ☐ Give your undivided attention to the caller
- ☐ Multi-task and talk to the person on the other end.
- ☐ Other: _____

You Are My Sister

What have you accomplished in your lifetime thus far?

1. _____

2. _____

3. _____

4. _____

5. _____

What are some of your fears and why?

1. _____

2. _____

3. _____

What are some of your insecurities?

1. _____

2. _____

3. _____

4. _____

5. _____

What are your strengths?

1. _____

2. _____

3. _____

4. _____

5. _____

What are some of your hobbies? (sports, reading, gardening, decorating, painting etc.)

_____

_____

_____

Which one of the following mostly describes you the most?

☐ Creative
☐ Analytical
☐ Structured
☐ Organized
☐ Unorganized
☐ None of the above

How do you make most of your daily decisions in your life?

- ☐ Emotional – your emotions drive your decisions.
- ☐ Spontaneous – you don't think about what you are doing, you just react.
- ☐ Planner – live by a plan and usually stick to it
- ☐ Thinker – usually think before you make an emotional or spontaneous decision.
- ☐ Other: _____

How often do you spend quiet time alone?

- ☐ Once a week
- ☐ Daily
- ☐ Monthly
- ☐ Never

How do you feel about yourself right now?

- ☐ Complete
- ☐ Incomplete

How do you manage your finances?

- ☐ Frugal
- ☐ Frivolous
- ☐ Investor
- ☐ Save
- ☐ Hoard
- ☐ Give

Anfra Boyd

Do you believe there is a heaven and a hell? Explain

☐ Yes   ☐ No

_____

_____

_____

Do you believe there is life after death/life? Explain

☐ Yes   ☐ No

_____

_____

_____

Do you sometimes feel that you have lived in another time or era? Explain

☐ Yes   ☐ No

_____

_____

Do you fear death or dying? Explain

☐ Yes   ☐ No

_____

_____

_____

Have you ever had a near death experience? Explain

☐ Yes   ☐ No

_____

_____

_____

When you were growing up, were you ever told how important it is to love yourself?

☐ Yes   ☐ No

Which one of the following applies to you?

☐   Independent
☐   Co-dependent
☐   Interdependent

- [ ] Self-Actualized
- [ ] Insecure
- [ ] Headstrong
- [ ] Other: _____

Which one of the following describes your childhood rearing?

- [ ] Two-parent family stable and loving home
- [ ] Single parent stable and loving home
- [ ] Foster care
- [ ] Grandparents
- [ ] Adoptive Parents
- [ ] Two-parent dysfunctional or divorced before 18
- [ ] Single parent unstable
- [ ] Stepparent, blended families
- [ ] Other: _____

Which one of following describes your family? (check all that apply)

- [ ] Loving, caring
- [ ] Dysfunctional
- [ ] Disjointed, distant
- [ ] Religious
- [ ] Hypocritical

What generational curses plague your family? (check all that apply)

- [ ] Alcoholism
- [ ] Teenage Pregnancy
- [ ] Drug abuse
- [ ] Mental Illness

You Are My Sister

- ☐ Family-secrets and lies
- ☐ Molestation
- ☐ Domestic Violence
- ☐ Incarceration
- ☐ Materialism
- ☐ Poverty
- ☐ Ignorance
- ☐ Adultery
- ☐ Incest
- ☐ Prostitution
- ☐ Homelessness
- ☐ Other: _____

What generational diseases plague your family? (check all that apply)

- ☐ Cancer
- ☐ Diabetes
- ☐ Sickle Cell Anemia
- ☐ Lupus
- ☐ Heart Disease
- ☐ Obesity
- ☐ High Blood Pressure
- ☐ Muscular Dystrophy
- ☐ Paranoid Schizophrenia   (Bi-Polar Disorder)
- ☐ Dyslexia
- ☐ Other: _____

What kind of thinker are you?

☐ Forward Thinker – One who is always thinking and planning ahead.

☐ Independent Thinker – One who asks questions and thinks for himself/herself before making a decision or conclusion.

☐ Co-dependent Thinker – One who usually depends on the thoughts and opinions of others before making a decision or conclusion.

☐ Critical Thinker – One who analyzes all point of views, statistics, and opinions of his or her own and others before making a decision or conclusion.

☐ Reactive Thinker - One who usually (does not think) and reacts to situations, circumstances or events before making a decision or conclusion.

Where are you on your journey of life?

☐ Headed in the right direction.

☐ Searching and trying to find my purpose

☐ At a stand still and don't know which way to go.

Which one of the following describes your financial status?

☐ Financially stable

☐ Drowning in Debt

☐ Living paycheck to paycheck

☐ Bankrupt

☐ Debt Free

☐ Other: _____

If you only had one choice, which one of the following would you choose?

☐ I would choose to spend the rest of my life with a man that is right for me.

☐ I would choose to spend the rest of my life wealthy and successful.

Why:

_____

_____

Which one of the following mostly describes you?

☐ Achiever   ☐ Over-Achiever   ☐ Under-Achiever

What are some of your fears? (check all that apply)

☐ Commitment   ☐ Loneliness ☐ Flying   ☐ Crowds

☐ Heights   ☐ Darkness   ☐ Debt   ☐ Success

☐ Failure   ☐ Parenting   ☐ Aging   ☐ The Future

☐ The Past   ☐ Marriage   ☐ Divorce   ☐ Heartache

Life Lessons

On your journey of life what lessons have you learned?

When going out with friends drive your own car
☐ Yes, I've learned   ☐ No, I haven't learned

To always practice safe sex
☐ Yes, I've learned   ☐ No, I haven't learned

Financial debt is bondage
☐ Yes, I've learned   ☐ No, I haven't learned

If a man cheats on his wife he will cheat on you
☐ Yes, I've learned   ☐ No, I haven't learned

How to save
☐ Yes, I've learned   ☐ No, I haven't learned

That knowledge is power
☐ Yes, I've learned   ☐ No, I haven't learned

To pay bills on time
☐ Yes, I've learned   ☐ No, I haven't learned

How to invest
☐ Yes, I've learned   ☐ No, I haven't learned

Everything that glitters is not gold
☐ Yes, I've learned   ☐ No, I haven't learned

Beauty and good looks are deceiving
☐ Yes, I've learned   ☐ No, I haven't learned

If a man hits you once he will hit you again
☐ Yes, I've learned   ☐ No, I haven't learned

You Are My Sister

What I want is not always what I need
      ☐ Yes, I've learned   ☐ No, I haven't learned

Not to date married men
      ☐ Yes, I've learned   ☐ No, I haven't learned

What goes around comes back around even harder
      ☐ Yes, I've learned   ☐ No, I haven't learned

You can never tell one lie
      ☐ Yes, I've learned   ☐ No, I haven't learned

Good sex is not good love
      ☐ Yes, I've learned   ☐ No, I haven't learned

Reading is fundamental
      ☐ Yes, I've learned   ☐ No, I haven't learned

That no one can love me better than I can
      ☐ Yes, I've learned   ☐ No, I haven't learned

It's better to give than to receive
      ☐ Yes, I've learned   ☐ No, I haven't learned

To let go of things that I can't change
      ☐Yes, I've learned   ☐ No, I haven't learned

To move on when a relationship is over
      ☐ Yes, I've learned   ☐ No, I haven't learned

It never pays to get revenge
      ☐ Yes, I've learned   ☐ No, I haven't learned

That ignorance is bliss
☐ Yes, I've learned   ☐ No, I haven't learned

When to speak up and when to keep silent
☐ Yes, I've learned   ☐ No, I haven't learned

Bigger is not always better
☐ Yes, I've learned   ☐ No, I haven't learned

Less is more
☐ Yes, I've learned   ☐ No, I haven't learned

The truth will indeed set you free
☐ Yes, I've learned   ☐ No, I haven't learned

That you don't need a leader to follow God
☐ Yes, I've learned   ☐ No, I haven't learned

That I have the power in my life
☐ Yes, I've learned   ☐ No, I haven't learned

To let go with love
☐ Yes, I've learned   ☐ No, I haven't learned

My body is my temple and to keep it scared
☐ Yes, I've learned   ☐ No, I haven't learned

To give without bragging or boasting about it
☐ Yes, I've learned   ☐ No, I haven't learned

To think before I speak
☐ Yes, I've learned   ☐ No, I haven't learned

You Are My Sister

To practice what I preach
    ☐ Yes, I've learned   ☐ No, I haven't learned

Money can't buy happiness
    ☐ Yes, I've learned   ☐ No, I haven't learned

The best things in life are free
    ☐ Yes, I've learned   ☐ No, I haven't learned

I can do bad all by myself
    ☐ Yes, I've learned   ☐ No, I haven't learned

I rather been alone than unhappy
    ☐ Yes, I've learned   ☐ No, I haven't learned

That being alone doesn't mean I'm lonely
    ☐ Yes, I've learned   ☐ No, I haven't learned

That real love doesn't break your heart
    ☐ Yes, I've learned   ☐ No, I haven't learned

If a man cheated once, he'll cheat again
    ☐ Yes, I've learned   ☐ No, I haven't learned

That I can forgive and leave at the same time
    ☐ Yes, I've learned   ☐ No, I haven't learned

There is a Higher Power in my life
    ☐ Yes, I've learned   ☐ No, I haven't learned

I don't need a man to make me feel complete or feminine
☐ Yes, I've learned   ☐ No, I haven't learned

That I can't have a baby with every man that I fall in love with
☐ Yes, I've learned   ☐ No, I haven't learned

If someone can make me happy they can make me sad
☐ Yes, I've learned   ☐ No, I haven't learned

Who Are You?
Describe how you feel about your life, the choices you've made and the direction you are headed.

_____

_____

_____

_____

_____

_____

_____

_____

Spiritual Journey

I hope that this spiritual journey has taken your mind and spirit to new heights of intuition, wisdom, and enlightenment. As we travel together on the road of spiritual consciousness and empowerment, I pray that we continue to laugh together, cry together and most of all grow together and continue to share our love of life, which is the love of God.

Like any journey there will always be detours, setbacks, delays and procrastination. Please remember that our journey is a continuous process of spiritual evolution, and we all are *"a work in progress."* So, wherever you are on your journey, periodically take time out to re-evaluate your priorities and check your road map to make sure you are still headed in the right direction. As you travel, hopefully, you'll become stronger, wiser and spiritually free. Always remember that you are only as strong as your greatest weakness. And that weakness is bound to cross your path time and time again as you travel along life's highway. If you fall or yield to its temptation, always remember that you can dust yourself off and get back up again!

Until the next book, I wish you peace and prosperity, joy and happiness and most of all a love that is everlasting – *Self-Love!*

Thanks-Giving

To my God, the Highest Power in the universe, I humbly say, "Thank you."

The last six years have been an exciting and joyous journey for me. I would like to thank all of the fans out there that have supported me on my spiritual journey. First of all, to all of the on-line readers who started out with me on this quest of spiritual enlightenment. Without you all spreading the word via emails, my books would not have been published. Thank you!

I would like to also thank the following book clubs and women's groups for your support as well: Neffertti Book Club in Memphis -- I love you all and thanks for your continued support, especially on the First African-American Book Club Summit Cruise.

The Good Book Club in Houston, TX - Pamela Walker-Williams and her crew. I had so much fun on the cruise. I'll see you on another cruise soon. Thanks for your support

To the Literati Book Club, Sisters of Literature, Zydeco Book Stars in Memphis. Raw Sisters Online Book club, Sister Sophisticate, The Bev Johnson Show @ WDIA in Memphis, Tracy Bethea & Christie Taylor @ Hallelujah FM in Memphis and Eileen "The Diva" at WDIA, You Are My Sister -- Thanks for your support.

To Andrea Echols and the ladies at Greater Middle Baptist Church. What a way to celebrate my fortieth birthday in Hot Springs Arkansas. Thank you soooooo much!

To MIFA-Opportunity Banc- Small business development staff: Amy Westerholm, Sharon Taylor McKinney, Carmen Mills and Toni McDivitt. Thank you for believing in me. My success is your success.

To April Thompson at News Channel 3 in Memphis, thank you for highlighting my story on your show. It was wonderful.

To my colleagues in the publishing industry: Pamela Williams Guinn, Maxine E. Thompson, Timmothy McCann, Margaret Johnson-Hodge, Rosalyn McMillan, Pat G'orge Walker, Norma Jarrett, Trisha Thomas, Kathleen Cross, Vincent Alexander, Victoria Christopher Murray, Sara Freeman-Smith and Lee Brock, your books have inspired my writing. I have enjoyed all of the book signings and events that we've shared.

To my cousin, sister and friend Cynthia Dortch, you have been my therapist, counselor, and strong shoulder to lean on. We are going to write that sketch comedy show as soon as I finish this book. We are going to make the world laugh!

I would also like to thank the following people for their support: Katrina McKinney, Angela Hale, Michelle Shelton, Denise Cunningham, Leroy Boyd, Jr., Maggie Wilson, Dorothy Bowman, Jerica Jones, Darryl Hegler, George Jones, and Wilbur Jones. Thank you for all of your support. I love you.

I would also like to say a very special thanks to Jae Basse at Triple B Productions for all of composing and formatting the CD for the book. May God bless you and your future.

To my parents Leroy and Beatrice Boyd, I love you very much and to my sisters Sarah Hilliard and Pamela Goodman.

Anfra

Different •Odd • Unique • Eloquent • Beautiful • Unforgettable

S ince the release of her first book titled *You Are My Sister: An Inspirational Book That Promotes Sisterhood and Spiritual Growth*, Anfra has become a highly sought after motivational speaker. Her message is simple "Know Thy Self."

As a poet, novelist and motivational speaker, she has traveled the country spreading her message of spiritual consciousness and empowerment. If your women's group, book club, church or social organization would like to book an engagement please contact: 901.353.BOOK (2665) or visit her website for more information.

Currently, Anfra is busy at work on her soon to be released novel titled *Blood Love*. To read excerpts of her books check out her website: www.youaremysister.com or email her at: MSANN2U@aol.com.